P9-BZE-923

TEDBooks

Also by Alan Lightman

The Accidental Universe: The World You Thought You Knew

Einstein's Dreams

Song of Two Worlds

The Diagnosis: A Novel

*The Discoveries: Great Breakthroughs in 20th-Century Science,
Including the Original Papers*

A Sense of the Mysterious: Science and the Human Spirit

Ancient Light: Our Changing View of the Universe

Origins: The Lives and Worlds of Modern Cosmologists

Reunion: A Novel

Mr g: A Novel

Good Benito: A Novel

Screening Room: A Memoir

In Praise of Wasting Time

ALAN LIGHTMAN

ILLUSTRATIONS BY DOLA SUN

TED Books
Simon & Schuster
New York London Toronto Sydney New Delhi

Simon & Schuster, Inc.
1230 Avenue of the Americas
New York, NY 10020

First TED Books hardcover edition May 2018

TED BOOKS and colophon are registered trademarks of TED Conferences, LLC.

SIMON & SCHUSTER and colophon are registered trademarks of Simon & Schuster, Inc.

For information about special discounts for bulk purchases, please contact Simon & Schuster Special Sales at 1-866-506-1949 or business@simonandschuster.com.

For information on licensing the TED Talk that accompanies this book, or other content partnerships with TED, please contact TEDBooks@TED.com.

Interior design by: MGMT.design
Jacket design by: MGMT.design
Interior illustrations by: Dola Sun

Manufactured in the United States of America
10 9 8 7 6 5 4 3 2 1

Library of Congress Cataloging-in-Publication Data is available.

ISBN 978-1-5011-5436-2
ISBN 978-1-5011-5437-9 (ebook)

To Bruce, Sheila, Ken, Mark, Getchen, Michael, Asia,
and my other friends in Alaska who have helped me
waste time in the most wonderful way

CONTENTS

In Praise of
Wasting Time

1 A Village in Cambodia

Not long ago, I found myself in a small village in a remote area of Cambodia. Many rural areas in the world have modern plumbing, electric ovens, satellite TVs, and other such technological conveniences, but not this one. The inhabitants of Tramung Chrum live in one-room huts without electricity or running water. Dangling light bulbs in the huts are powered by car batteries. Food is cooked over open fires. The villagers support themselves by growing rice, watermelons, and cucumbers. Their religion is a version of moderate Islam, called Imam San Cham, combined with animism. When someone needs healing, the villagers perform a ceremony in which they summon the spirits of ancestors, monkeys, and horses. The ghosts inhabit the bodies of the villagers, who dance wildly through the night. Other than these moments, the villagers go about their lives in quiet calm. They rise with the sun. After breakfast, they herd their cows out for grazing, then walk to the rice fields and tend to their crops. They return to their huts as the light starts to dim and gather firewood for cooking the evening meal.

Each morning, the women ride their bicycles on a rutted red dirt road to a market ten miles away to trade for goods and food they cannot grow themselves. Through a translator, I asked one of the women how long the daily trip took. She gave me a puzzled look and said, "I never thought about that."

I was startled at her disinterest in time. And envious. We in the "developed" world have created a frenzied lifestyle in which not a minute is to be wasted. The precious twenty-four hours of each day are carved up, dissected, and reduced to ten-minute units of efficiency. We become agitated and angry in the waiting room of a doctor's office if we've been sitting for ten minutes or more. We grow impatient if our laser printers don't spit out at least five pages per minute. And we must be connected to the grid at all times. We take our smartphones and laptops with us on vacation. We go through our email at restaurants. Or our online bank accounts while walking in the park. The teenagers I know (and some of their parents) check their smartphones at least every five minutes of their "free" waking hours. At night, many sleep with their phones on their chests or next to their beds. When the school day ends, our children are loaded with piano lessons and dance classes and soccer games and extra language classes. Our university curricula are so crammed that our young people don't have time to digest and reflect on the material they are supposed to be learning.

I plead guilty myself. If I take the time to examine my own twenty-four hours per day, here's what I find: from the instant I open my eyes in the morning until I turn out the lights at night, I am at work on some project. First thing in the morning,

I check my email. For any unexpected opening of time that appears during the day, I rush to patch it, as if a tear in my trousers. I find a project, indeed I feel compelled to find a project, to fill up the hole. If I have an extra hour, I can work at my laptop on an article or class lesson. If I have a few minutes, I can answer a letter or read an online news story. With only seconds, I can check phone messages. Unconsciously, without thinking about it, I have subdivided my day into smaller and smaller units of efficient time use, until there are no holes left, no breathing spaces remaining. I rarely goof off. I rarely follow a path that I think might lead to a dead end. I rarely "waste" time. And certainly, I would never ever spend a couple of hours of each day going to the market without knowing exactly how long the trip took and figuring out how to listen to an audiobook on the way.

It's not only me. All around me, I feel a sense of urgency, a vague fear of not being plugged in, a fear of not keeping up. I feel like Josef K. in Kafka's *The Trial*, who lives in a world of ubiquitous suspicion and powerful but invisible authority. Yet there is no authority here, only a pervasive mentality.

I can remember a time when I did not live in this way. I can remember those days of my childhood when I would slowly walk home from school by myself and take long detours through the woods. With the silence broken only by the sound of my own footsteps, I would follow turtles as they lumbered down a dirt path. Where were they going, and why? I would build play forts out of fallen trees. I would sit on the banks of Cornfield Pond and waste hours watching tadpoles in the shallows or the sway of water grasses in the wind. My mind meandered. I thought about what I wanted for dinner that night, whether God was a man or a woman, whether tadpoles knew they were destined to become frogs, what it would feel like to be dead, what I wanted to be when I became a man, the fresh bruise on my knee. When the light began fading, I wandered home.

I ask myself: What happened to those careless, wasteful hours at the pond? How has the world changed? Of course, part of the answer is simply that I grew up. Adulthood undeniably brings responsibilities and career pressures and a certain awareness of the weight of life. Yet that is only part of what has happened. Indeed, an enormous transformation has occurred in the world from the 1950s and '60s of my youth to today. A transformation so vast that it has altered all that we say and do and think, yet often in ways so subtle and ubiquitous that we are hardly aware of them. Among other things, the world today is faster, more scheduled, more fragmented, less patient, louder, more wired, more public. For want of a better phrase, I will call this world "the wired world." By this term, I do not mean only digital communication, the Internet, and social media. I also mean the frenzied pace and noise of the world.

There are many different aspects of today's time-driven, wired existence, but they are connected. All can be traced to recent technological advances and economic prosperity in a

complex web of cause and effect. Throughout history, the pace of life has always been fueled by the speed of communication. The speed of communication, in turn, has been central to the technological advance that has led to the Internet, social media, and the vast and all-consuming network that I simply call "the grid." That same technology has also been part of the general economic progress that has increased productivity in the workplace, which, when coupled with the time-equals-money equation, has led to a heightened awareness of the commercial and goal-oriented uses of time—at the expense of the more reflective, free-floating, and non-goal-oriented uses of time.

Technology, however, is only a tool. Human hands work the tool. Behind the technology, I believe that our entire way of thinking has changed, our way of being in the world, our social and psychological ethos. Many of us cannot spend an hour of unscheduled time, cannot sit alone in a room for ten minutes without external stimulation, cannot take a walk in the woods without a smartphone. This behavioral syndrome is part of the noisy, hyperconnected, splintered, and high-speed matrix of the wired world.

Clearly, the recent technological and economic developments have been beneficial in many ways. Vast amounts of medical information about symptoms, diagnoses, and treatments are instantly available through the Internet to doctors in remote areas. Family members who are separated by great distance can see and talk to each other as if they were in the same room. With more speed and productivity, we are richer. We have more food and better houses. We have more cars, telephones, electric ranges and blenders, vacuum cleaners, dishwashers, microwaves and refrigerators, televisions, iPhones and iPods and iPads, CD players and DVD players, humidifiers, copying machines, air conditioners and heaters. My own work as a scientist, writer, and social entrepreneur has profited enormously from the recent technological advances. I can do research online and scan through mountains of facts that, in the past, would have required that I travel to distant libraries or have articles and information mailed to me through the post. For a number of years, I have been overseeing a project in Southeast Asia for the advancement of young women, a project I could never have undertaken without quick communication between my desk in Concord, Massachusetts, and my second office in Phnom Penh. I much admire the technologies and individuals who have made my life possible. But these developments have come at a cost. And it is time that we recognize what we have lost.

What exactly have we lost? If we are so crushed by our schedules, to-do lists, and hyperconnected media that we no longer have moments to think and reflect on both ourselves and the world, what have we lost? If we cannot sit alone in a quiet room with only our thoughts for ten minutes, what have we lost? If we no longer have time to let our minds wander and roam without particular purpose, what have we lost?

If we and our children no longer have time to play? If we no longer experience the quality of slowness, or a digestible rate of information, or silence, or privacy? More narrowly, what have I personally lost when I must be engaged with a project every hour of the day, when I rarely let my mind spin freely without friction or deadlines, when I rarely sever myself from the rush and the heave of the external world—what have I lost?

Certainly, I have threatened my creative activities. Psychologists have long known that creativity thrives on unstructured time, on play, on "divergent thinking," on unpurposed ramblings through the mansions of life. Gustav Mahler routinely took three- or four-hour walks after lunch, stopping to jot down ideas in his notebook. Carl Jung did his most creative thinking and writing when he took time off from his frenzied practice in Zurich and went to his country house in Bollingen. In the middle of a writing project, Gertrude Stein wandered about the countryside looking at cows. Einstein, in his 1949 autobiography, described how his thinking involved letting his mind roam over many possibilities and making connections between concepts previously unconnected. All unscheduled. "For me it is unquestionable that our thinking goes on . . . to a considerable degree unconsciously," he wrote. Don't we need empty spaces for such mental adventures?

I have also endangered the needed *replenishment* of mind that comes from doing nothing in particular, from taking long walks without destination, from simply finding a few moments of quiet away from the noise of the world. The mind needs to rest. The mind needs periods of calm. Such a need has been recognized for thousands of years. It was described as early as 1500 BCE in the meditation traditions of Hinduism. And later in Buddhism. A passage from the Buddhist Dhammapada reads: "When a monk has gone into an empty place, and has calmed his mind, [he] experiences a delight that transcends that of men."

But I've lost more. I believe I have lost something of my inner self. By inner self, I mean that part of me that imagines, that dreams, that explores, that is constantly questioning who I am and what is important to me. My inner self is my true freedom. My inner self roots me to me, and to the ground beneath me. The sunlight and soil that nourish my inner self are solitude and personal reflection. When I listen to my inner self, I hear the breathing of my spirit. Those breaths are so tiny and delicate, I need stillness to hear them, I need slowness to hear them. I need vast, silent spaces in my mind. I need privacy. Without the breathing and the voice of my inner self, I am a prisoner of the wired world around me.

2 The Grid

On the cover of the November 7, 2016, issue of *Time* is a picture of a teenage girl. She has shoulder-length dark hair, is wearing jeans and a lace-up pink shirt. Her arms droop at her sides. She looks like all the life has been drained out of her, like she has no hope left in the world. For all of us with children, we think, *Please let my child never be so.* Next to the teenager is the headline: "Anxiety, Depression and the American Adolescent."

Of course, teenagers throughout time have been sulky and sullen. But this is something else, something new. The number of "distressed" young people in America is dramatically rising. According to the National Institute of Mental Health, from 2010 to 2015 the fraction of adolescents (ages twelve to seventeen) who reported at least one major depressive episode in the previous year increased from around eight percent to almost thirteen percent. There are, of course, many factors contributing to this epidemic. But some experts say that the main driver is the massive and pervasive presence of the digital grid, with little opportunity or desire to disconnect.

The grid replaces in-the-flesh reality with virtual reality, and that virtual reality is loud, all-consuming, dehumanizing, and relentless. It can drown out the rest of life. And it rushes ahead, without waiting for anyone. Janis Whitlock, director of the Cornell Research Program on Self-Injury and Recovery, says that our young people are "in a cauldron of stimulus they can't get away from, or don't want to get away from, or don't know how to get away from." According to a recent Pew survey, the average American teenager today sends or receives more than 110 text messages a day. A 2015 study of social-media use of thirteen-year-olds, conducted by researchers at the University of California (Davis) and the University of Texas (Dallas), found that "there is no firm line between their real and online worlds." A big difference between the digital screens of today and the televisions of the 1950s is that in those days your parents could turn off the darn thing. Not so easy today, when a large fraction of young people have their own digital devices.

So what's the problem with nonstop stimulation? Ross Peterson, a New England psychiatrist who has treated dozens of teenage patients, told me that in his view the source of increased depression and anxiety in teenagers is their "terror of aloneness." That terror, in turn, is intimately connected to the intense hyperconnected social-media environment of today. Modern teenagers, who live on the virtual planets of Facebook and Snapchat and Instagram, find it nearly impossible to be alone. They are always connected. Peterson mentioned to me the acronym FOMO, which stands for "Fear of Missing Out." And what are we missing out on if we aren't intravenously connected to the grid? The vast, squirming, unceasing, ubiquitous explosion of images and words, stories, messages and tweets, provocations, real news and fake news, happenings, and connections that is the Internet. The grid. It's an addiction. We can get another hit with just the push of a button. And like any drug addiction, there's never enough. We are dependent on the digital flow. We are always waiting for the next hit. We are always running to catch up. We are always behind. FOMO.

Associated with Peterson's "terror of aloneness" and FOMO is plain loneliness. In her new book *iGen*, psychologist Jean Twenge quotes research by a Monitoring the Future survey showing that the percentage of eighth, tenth, and twelfth graders agreeing with the statement "A lot of times I feel lonely" underwent a dramatic increase beginning in 2007, around the time the iPhone was first released, and has not come down. (And, according to a 2017 survey by investment firm Piper Jaffray, seventy-six percent of teens today own an iPhone.) Twenge asked her undergraduate students at San Diego State University what they do with their smartphones when they sleep. Nearly all of them sleep with their smartphones beside them in bed, under their pillows, or within easy reach. They check social media right before going to sleep and right after waking up. One of the students said: "I know

I shouldn't, but I just can't help it." Those are the words of addiction.

Modern communication technology has shaped our understanding of the world, our self-identity, our sense of personal worth, our relationships, even our sense of time and space. As my MIT colleague psychologist Sherry Turkle writes in her book *Alone Together,* "Technology proposes itself as the architect of our intimacies." Leonora, a fifty-seven-year-old chemistry professor in Turkle's study, says: "I use e-mail to make appointments to see friends, but I'm so busy that I'm often making an appointment one or two months in the future. After we set things up by e-mail, we do not call. Really. I don't call. They don't call. . . . What do I feel? I feel I have 'taken care of that person.' " Audrey, a sixteen-year-old high school student, told Turkle: "Making an [online] avatar and texting. Pretty much the same. . . . You're creating your own little ideal person and sending it out. . . . You can write anything about yourself; these people don't know. You can create who you want to be. . . . [M]aybe in real life it won't work for you, you can't pull it off. But you can pull it off on the Internet." Surveys show that since the advent of the iPhone in 2007, young people spend less time dating and less time in person-to-person meetings with friends. Instead, they curl up at home and relate to the world through their digital devices.

A few years ago, I went out to dinner with my then twenty-five-year-old daughter and her friends. As soon as they sat down, the young women placed their smartphones on the table, like miniature oxygen tanks carried everywhere by emphysema patients. Every minute or two, one or the other of them glanced down at her device to see what new messages had arrived and to send out other messages. Occasionally, a factual question would come up as they talked. Conversation stopped, while somebody dove into the Internet and fetched the answer. And what of their sense of time? The world for them has been chopped up into two-minute segments between hits on the Internet. This disembodied and wired existence is no doubt familiar. It's our new reality. For the younger generations, and some of the older as well, this relation to the world is simply the natural order of things. Yet I did not feel like I was sitting at a table with my daughter and her friends, as I did twenty years earlier. Rather, I felt like I had been digitized myself, that we were all megabytes being streamed through the Web. Spoken words and facial expressions were just two channels among many. And even though my daughter and her friends were together at the table, they were not together. They were not truly there.

To the anxious and depressed American adolescent on the cover of *Time*, the Internet is infinite. There's no way a teenager, or any of us, can keep up with it, keep up even with the avalanche of postings by our own friends. Inevitably, we will suffer from FOMO. We will always be missing out. And since the digital screen has replaced reality and has become

the architect of our intimacies, we will always fear aloneness. We will find it next to impossible to sit in a quiet room by ourselves and figure out who we are. The biggest thing we're missing out on is, in fact, ourselves.

Am I exaggerating? Is it truly impossible to sit alone in a quiet room for a few minutes without external stimulation in today's world? Try it out yourself. A couple of years ago, some psychologists at the University of Virginia and Harvard tried it out with college students. Each of their 146 subjects was required to sit in a chair, alone, in a quiet room for twelve minutes. All external devices, including smartphones and watches, were confiscated. However, one type of external stimulation was allowed. A button next to the chair, when pushed, would administer an electric shock to the participant. Before the experiment began, the participants were asked to press the button "just for practice." All of them reported that the shock was unpleasant, something they would avoid if at all possible. Then the experiment began. One at a time, the subjects were asked to sit "for ten or twenty minutes" (exactly how long they didn't know, since their devices had been taken from them), with two rules: They couldn't fall asleep, and they couldn't get out of the chair. But if they wanted to press the button and get shocked, that was okay. The researchers found that sixty-seven percent of the men and twenty-five percent of the women chose to shock themselves during the twelve minutes of the experiment rather than sit quietly with their thoughts.

Shocks come in many forms, of course. The constant stimulation and noise and multitasking of the grid offer a steady
stream of shocks, and we have grown accustomed to these
shocks. In fact, in some bizarre way, our bodies and brains
may have been altered so that we may actually *need* these
shocks and disturbances to function, like a drug dependency.
In her book *Distracted*, Maggie Jackson has documented the
many distractions in today's world and concluded that we are
no longer able to "pay attention" to anything. Paying attention
to one thing too long seems to make us uncomfortable
and nervous. In an article titled "No Task Left Behind?
Examining the Nature of Fragmented Work," psychologists
and information scientists at the University of California
(Irvine) report finding that workers switch tasks *every three
minutes* during their workday. That's the Internet. In a vicious
cycle, that constant interruption may be something that
we need in our habituated dependency on stimulation and
distraction, causing more stress and distraction, leading to
greater dependency.

I have a confession to make. I bought a smartphone—four
months ago at the time of this writing. I have succumbed.

If I remember correctly, the first cell phones were available
in the mid-1980s. Until very recently, I owned only a flip
phone. Flip phones make phone calls, and that's all that mine
did, like a hammer that only hammers. Even a flip phone
I was reluctant to get, fearing that it might interrupt me

wherever I was and whatever I was doing, but my wife wanted to be in frequent contact with me when I traveled. When smartphones first became prevalent, somewhere around the year 2000, I noticed how they dominated the lives of their owners—stealing quiet time and solitude and mediating all experience—and I vowed never to own such a diabolical device. My wife got a smartphone. My friends got smartphones. My daughters got smartphones. People chided me.

One night last summer, I was driving my boat to my island home in Maine in a dense fog, and I got lost. With me were my wife, my two daughters, my son-in-law, and my three-year-old granddaughter. I can navigate the waters near my island home on clear nights, or in a fog in the daytime, but the combination of darkness and fog is a nearly insurmountable challenge. All you can see with a flashlight or even a nautical floodlight is a glowing white cocoon surrounded by blackness. I was terrified of running into rocks or wandering out into open water, and my fear was felt by all my passengers. After a few minutes of fright, my son-in-law took out his smartphone, pushed a couple of buttons, and on the screen magically appeared a map of the area, with a throbbing dot indicating precisely where our boat was. Using the device, we then easily navigated our way through the fog to the island and my dock.

Then and there, I decided I had to own a smartphone. But I promised myself I would use it only for calls and navigation. I bought the phone. A few weeks later, I found myself in an unfamiliar neighborhood in an unfamiliar city, in need of a taxi, and I used my smartphone to contact a digital ride service. I felt a pang of guilt. But it was so easy. I didn't have to give a fumbled description of my location to a dispatcher. The disembodied grid immediately knew where I was. A few days after that, I heard a beep from my smartphone and saw a message waiting from my oldest daughter, who lives several hundred miles away. Attached to the message was a video of my granddaughter in a dance recital earlier that day. I dictated (yes, dictated) into the phone a reply to my daughter and granddaughter, a message they received a few seconds later. I remember what I was feeling at that moment. Was I feeling that I had lost my quiet and privacy and contemplative space? No, I was feeling joy at seeing my granddaughter wiggle her hips to the music, dressed in tiny toe shoes and pink tights. Another day, I was sitting in an airport, waiting for a flight. I could have read a book or written in my journal, as was my custom when waiting for an extended period. My smartphone was lodged within a zippered pocket of my carry-on bag, only four feet away. I could see its outline against the fabric of the bag. Should I get out my journal and write about my experiences the previous day? I wasn't actively thinking about the smartphone. But I knew it was there. It had been several hours since I had last checked my email. Might there be important messages waiting for me that needed immediate reply? All these thoughts were hazy, almost unconscious, like an old bruise that you don't notice. Without thinking, without having made any conscious decision, I unzipped the pocket, took out the phone, and checked my email.

And so it goes. Against my will, knowing all the dangers, I have been sucked into the maelstrom. I have heard the song of the Sirens and succumbed. I should have tied myself to the mast.

3 The Rush and the Heave

A momentous study by the University of Hertfordshire in collaboration with the British Council found that the *walking speed* of pedestrians in thirty-two cities around the world increased by ten percent just in the ten-year period from 1995 to 2005.

How did we arrive at this point in the history of the world?

First, there's business. The pace of life has always been driven by the pace of business, and the pace of business has always been driven by the speed of communication. In 1881, in a book titled *American Nervousness, its Causes and Consequences*, physician George Beard noted the increase in "nervousness" and stress in the public caused by the new communication technologies of the day: the railroad and the telegraph. Today, it's the Internet. When the telegraph was invented in the nineteenth century, information could be transmitted at the rate of about four bits per second. By 1985, near the beginnings of the public Internet, the rate was about a thousand bits per second. Today, the rate is about one billion bits per second. A friend of mine who has been practicing law for thirty years wrote to me that her "mental capacity to receive, synthesize, and thoughtfully complete a legal document has been outpaced by technology." She says that with the advent of e-mail, her clients want immediate turnaround, even on complex matters, and the practice of law has been "forever changed from a reasoning profession to a marathon." Another friend who works at a major software company described to me the "efficient" job interview process at his firm. An applicant is interviewed independently by several people on the selection committee. Afterward, there are no face-to-face meetings of the committee to discuss the applicant. Instead, each interviewer, within twenty minutes of completing the interview, must write up his or her impressions and send them by e-mail to the other members of the committee. If the transmission of judgment isn't completed within this time frame, that interviewer is out of the loop. Other business presses on.

Much of the pace and stress of the workplace, which eventually carries over to the rest of life, is caused by the relationship between time and money. Since the Industrial Revolution and the use of time to measure labor, we in the developed world have embraced the adage that time is money. Fifty years ago, the economist Gary S. Becker made an explicit analysis of the "cost of time" in households by putting work time and non-work time on an equal footing. That is, different kinds of leisure time were assigned a value when comparing them to working time that is paid for. One of Becker's intuitively obvious conclusions is that people will spend less time on various leisure activities when their work (paid) time becomes more profitable. And, with our advancing technology, work time has indeed become more profitable. We are more and more productive. On average, each hour of labor produces more goods than it did in the past. According to the Bureau of Labor Statistics, productivity has more than *quadrupled* since 1950. It's no wonder that Harry Triandis, a social psychologist emeritus at the University of Illinois, says that the time-equals-money equation, when combined with the higher productivity afforded by high-speed communication, "creates an urgency to make every moment count." When the time-equals-money equation is combined with the power of the grid, we see Becker's predictions in action. A recent survey of 483 professionals reported in the *Harvard Business Review* found that sixty percent of those who carry smartphones are connected to their jobs 13.5 hours or more each day on weekdays and five hours on weekends. That's seventy-two hours per week. Technology and economic progress, instead of increasing leisure time (including "wasted time"), have done just the opposite.

We find an extreme example of the time-equals-money equation and its repercussions in the legal profession. The notorious "billable hour" employed by law firms, instituted to ensure that every minute of their lawyers' time is profitable, carves billable office time down to increments as small as 0.1 hour. That's six minutes. A study by legal scholar M. Cathleen Kaveny, now at Boston College, suggests that awareness of the monetary value of their time is a major factor in the mental state of lawyers. She begins her report in the *Loyola University Chicago Law Journal* with the statement: "Many lawyers are very unhappy, particularly lawyers who work in big firms. They may be rich, and getting even richer, but they are also miserable, or so they say." Then she goes on to explore the reason why.

On a practical level, the inexorable demands of the billable hour are responsible for many of the most unpleasant aspects of life in a large law firm, including the growing pressure on lawyers (particularly young associates) to work even longer hours. I believe, however, that this way of calculating the value of legal work does more subtle and more serious damage to the attorneys forced to bow to its demands than that inflicted by overwork. The regime of the billable hour presupposes a distorted and harmful account of the meaning and purpose of a lawyer's time, and therefore, the meaning and purpose of a lawyer's life, which, after all, is lived in and through time. The account, which ultimately reduces the value of time to money, is deeply inimical to human flourishing.

The urgency to make every moment count has affected all aspects of life. It permeates our thoughts, our daily routines, our meals, our vacations, our family time, our relationship with our children. It becomes the air we breathe. It puts walls around our mental and psychic space. It even affects our ability to enjoy pleasurable experiences. In a fascinating experiment done by social scientists Sanford E. DeVoe and

Julian House of the University of Toronto, college students were asked questions about their jobs and annual incomes. A control group then listened to the first part of "The Flower Duet" from the opera *Lakmé*. An experimental group was asked to calculate their hourly wage before listening to the same music. Immediately following the music, participants were asked "to what extent are you happy right now?" and scored their happiness on a scale ranging from "Not at all happy" to "Very happy." Participants who were not asked to first compute their hourly wage were significantly happier after listening to the music. DeVoe and House concluded that "the impatience that results from placing a price on time impairs individuals' ability to derive happiness from pleasurable experiences."

Consider the crammed schedules, speed of appointments, jobs, getting and spending, pressure and stress of the lives of our young people and students. Surveys show a trend of increasing stress among college students similar to the increase in depression among teens. According to a survey by the Associated Press and mtvU, the number of college students who said they had experienced stress in the previous few months increased by twenty percent from 2003 and 2008. A survey of over 350,000 students at 683 colleges by UCLA's Higher Education Institute found that the stress among college freshmen has been increasing since 1985, when the surveys began. According to UCLA professor of education Linda J. Sax, "This [trend] is a reflection of an increasingly fast-paced society, made more so by computers and other media." McKenna Bulkley, a journalism student at the University of Missouri, recently described her life this way:

> Here's a quick look into a normal day for me: Wake up, eat (maybe), drink coffee, go to class for a few hours. Maybe squeeze in an hour or two at my on-campus job or do some homework, and then grab a quick lunch and maybe some coffee before I go to job #2. Then I get to spend seven hours there, and when I get home I do homework until who knows when. The next day, I get to wake up tired and do it all over again. Or if I'm lucky and it's the weekend, I can grab an extra shift at work or catch up on the homework I didn't get a chance to do earlier in the week. Somewhere in there I usually try to find the time to spend a few minutes with my friends once or twice a week or at the very least watch some Netflix in order to preserve my sanity. . . . And the thing is, I know very few college students who don't have schedules like mine. Even if they're fortunate enough to not have to work, our schedules are loaded with extracurriculars and internships—anything to pad our résumés for after graduation. Of course we're Generation Stress. We have to be.

In an article titled "Overloaded with information, students need critical thinking skills," published in *University World News*, Adam Peck writes that students today are "deluged" with information. Yet "despite the tremendous educational potential of the information age, students seem to be less prepared to critically evaluate information or determine and defend what they believe." Little wonder. When do they have time to reflect on what they have learned? Certainly Ms. Bulkley does not.

The ethos of schedule and speed has penetrated even the lives of our youngest children. Here's what writer Rachel Garlinghouse says about the lives of children today: "Like many parents, I feel an immense amount of pressure. Pressure to make sure my kids can count to ten in Mandarin by toddlerhood. Pressure to help my children find out where they are most talented by the time they are in kindergarten in order to make sure they practice (at least five nights a week) the skills necessary to excel in that particular area. . . . Pressure to make sure they are in at least four activities during any given season to ensure their success in life."

I cannot imagine many children today who could take a few hours wandering home from school as I did in my childhood, wasting hours watching tadpoles in the shallows or the sway of water grasses in the wind. My own children certainly did not. Their afternoons were filled with scheduled sports and extracurricular lessons of various kinds. My children are now adults, married, grappling with the harried lives of *their* children. My four-year-old granddaughter has already learned how to push buttons on smartphones and connect to the grid.

It has all happened so quickly. Fifty years ago, the Internet didn't exist. Twenty-five years ago, Google didn't exist. While all this progress has been taking place, we have not been paying attention. (And how could we, with all the distractions?) We have let ourselves be pushed along by the wave of technology and prosperity without looking to see where we are going. Little by little, our world has been transformed. Little by little, we have lost the silences, the needed time for contemplation, the open spaces in our minds, the privacies we once had. We have lost the knowledge of who we are and what is important to us. All of it happening so gradually and compellingly that we haven't noticed. It is as if we have gone deaf. And even now, most of us do not notice that we can't hear anymore. We accept the world as it is.

I live less than a mile from Walden Pond. There, in the woods on the east side of the pond, Henry David Thoreau built his small cabin and later wrote his great book. Some days, but not often enough, I manage to pry myself loose from the rush and the heave for a couple of hours and take a quiet walk around the pond. It is a winding dirt trail, a little narrower than the dirt road followed by the women of Tramung Chrum. In the winter, the air is crisp and sharp. In the summer, it is soft and aromatic. In winter, I am usually the only one on the trail. The world is silent and white, and the pond is sometimes frozen over. All I can hear is the crunching of my boots in the snow. In the spring, ducks swim in the pond. I listen to the calls of the blackbirds and chickadees and kingfishers and red-tailed hawks. "Our life is frittered away by detail," wrote Thoreau. "Simplicity, simplicity, simplicity. I say, let your affairs be as two or three, and not a hundred or a thousand." I want to recover what I have lost. I want to live in the slow world. I want to be free. Yet I feel the invisible cage. Even as I walk around the pond, the electromagnetic waves of the Internet rush through my body. Technology is both blessing and curse. In Thoreau's day, the new technology was the railroad. "We do not ride on the railroad," wrote Thoreau, "it rides upon us." Can I escape? Can I find stillness? A leaf falls from a tree. Slowly, so slowly, I watch it stop time.

4 Play

When I was in grade school and high school, I loved to build things.

I loved to experiment. Most of my experiments I conducted in a little laboratory I created in a large closet off my second-floor bedroom. In my homemade alchemist's den, I hoarded resistors and capacitors, coils of wire of various thicknesses and grades, batteries, switches, photoelectric cells, magnets, dangerous chemicals that I had secretly ordered from unsuspecting supply stores, test tubes and petri dishes, lovely glass flasks, Bunsen burners, scales. I delighted in my equipment. I remember building a "carbide cannon." To make it, I welded a spark plug into one end of a tennis ball can, with wires leading from the contacts of the spark plug to my battery a safe distance away. After which I put some calcium carbide and water in the open end of the can and corked it. An explosive gas formed. Then, I fired the spark plug. The cannon made a monstrously loud bang, which could be heard all over the neighborhood.

Another project was a rocket, with a lizard passenger. I mixed my own rocket fuel. A fuel that burns too fast will explode like a bomb; a fuel that burns too slowly will fizzle like a barbecue grill. What I wanted was the right proportions of sulfur, charcoal, and potassium nitrate (all harmless individually but not in combination). At apogee, the capsule containing the lizard astronaut was ejected by a small charge of gunpowder, ignited by a mercury switch of my design. The capsule then floated back to earth attached to a parachute.

On some of my adventures, I had a school friend named John, a year older than me. Weekends, we would lie around his room or mine, bored, listening to Bob Dylan records and occasionally thinking of things to excite our imaginations. Sometimes we walked to Clark and Faye's on Poplar Avenue, the best-stocked supply store in Memphis. There, we squandered whole Saturdays, adrift in the aisles of copper wire, socket wrenches, diodes and batteries, oddly shaped metallic brackets that we had no immediate use for but purchased anyway.

Our most successful collaboration was a light-borne communication device. The heart of the thing was a mouthpiece made out of the lid of a shoe polish can, with a section of a balloon stretched tightly across it. Onto this rubber membrane we attached a tiny piece of silvered glass, which acted as a mirror. A light beam was focused on the tiny mirror and reflected off it. When a person talked into the mouthpiece, the rubber vibrated. In turn, the tiny mirror quivered, and those quiverings produced a shimmering in the reflected beam, like the shimmering of sunlight reflected off a trembling lake. In that way, the information in the speaker's voice was precisely encoded onto light, each rise and dip of uttered sound translating itself into a brightening or dimming of light. When reflected, the fluttering beam traveled across John's cluttered bedroom to our receiver, which was built from largely off-the-shelf stuff: a photocell to convert varying intensities of light into varying intensities of electrical current, an amplifier, and a microphone. Finally, the original voice was reproduced on the other end.

There were many other creations. None of these projects were assigned in school. They were just things I did for fun in the long afternoons after school when I wasn't wandering about Cornfield Pond. In fact, it was often the case that I didn't have any definite project in mind. I just liked to mix chemicals and see what would happen. Or tinker with batteries and switches and wires. Many of my mixings and tinkerings didn't lead to anything. They were merely explorations of the world and the hidden paths in my mind. I was at play.

Looking back on these projects and non-projects now, I can see that they were part of the development of my imagination. They were part of the secret world I inhabited—not the world of my teachers, not the world of my parents, not the world of houses and customs and laws, but a world of my own. In fact, I think there was something slightly rebellious and even subversive about these projects—for the very reason that they were *not* assigned or required by any of the authorities in the world. (John and I never saved the directions that came with new parts. We much preferred to figure things out on our own by trial and error.) Unconsciously, I was distancing myself from the world of structure, rules, and scheduled activities and giving free rein to my thoughts. I was scientifically inclined, and the various projects I've described were projects of science, but other young people with different inclinations and time on their hands might create poems or songs or papier-mâché animals.

In various ways, the escape from structure and schedule, the indulgence in space without time, the development of one's inner world, and the full release of the imagination are all interconnected. The prominent New Zealand educator Brian Sutton-Smith, who spent his life studying play, believed that "the benefit play accords each child, who gains confidence in a variety of . . . pretense forms and thereby develops an inner, subjective life, [is] a life that becomes the child's own relatively private possession. . . . [T]he earliest pretend play . . . serves as the basis for their development of the duality of private and public that we adults take for granted."

In play, we live in a private world of our own creation. In play, rules are questioned, revised, or dispensed with altogether. Danish researcher Signe Juhl Møller and others have found that when children are playing, the meaning of a particular toy or object can change, leading to novel uses of the toy. "These perceptions and uses may violate the rules and norms outside or inside the play activity," says Møller. When we play, we are free. We are free of authority. We are free of the grid. We are free of time. And we are left to roam through the halls of our minds. Canadian educator Sister Valerie Van Cauwenberghe says: "Play is the total of all the spontaneous, creative activities in which children freely choose to engage. The urge to teach must not conflict with the desire to learn."

Our time-driven existence is diminishing the space for play and damaging our children. In a clinical report for the American Academy of Pediatrics, physician Kenneth R. Ginsburg writes that "Play allows children to use their creativity while developing their imagination, dexterity, and physical, cognitive, and emotional strength." Yet "[m]any . . . children are being raised in an increasingly hurried and pressured style that may limit the protective benefits they would gain from child-driven play." A similar conclusion has been reached by psychologists Kathy Hirsh-Pasek, Roberta Michnick Golinkoff, and others, who have found that the amount of time for free play in children's lives has decreased over the last few decades.

Sutton-Smith believed in the value of play for adults as well as for children. Activities just for fun and amusement. Time to let the mind rest. Time for daydreaming. Sometimes downright procrastination. A few years ago, Jihae Shin, an assistant professor of management and human resources at the business school of the University of Wisconsin (Madison), performed a simple experiment to test the impact of play and procrastination on creativity. Professor Shin asked people to come up with new business ideas. The participants were divided into three groups.

The first group started throwing out ideas immediately. The second group, before throwing out ideas, was asked to first spend a few minutes playing *Minesweeper* or *Solitaire*, two popular video games from the 1990s. An independent group of business people rated the ideas and found that those in the second group, who had "procrastinated" for a few minutes, were noticeably more creative. Furthermore, Shin determined that another group, asked to play the games *before* being given the assignment, was no more creative than the first group. Evidently, the decisive factor in increasing creativity seems to have been allowing a period of time to ponder a given problem at a leisurely and subconscious level, exploring possibilities while at play. Seeding the mind with a particular problem *before* play may be crucial. In such a case, what appears as procrastination or avoidance of the problem might in fact be a beneficial use of the mind. (I will have more to say about what one might call the "prepared" mind in the next chapter.) As Einstein said, a lot of good thinking and problem solving occurs at the unconscious level. For which we need space and time.

Animal researchers have long noted that all of the more intelligent animals engage in some form of play. Monkeys play. Kittens chase each other and paw at a hanging string. Sea lions will toss sticks to each other. Dolphins will stop what they are doing when a large boat approaches and ride in its bow wave. I was once in the ocean in a small sailboat when a dolphin not only swam alongside us but catapulted itself over the stern. A hilarious video on YouTube shows a few minutes in the lives of some young crows. At first, the birds appear bored. Then one of them spots a low-hanging branch on a tree, flies up and grabs the branch, and swings back and forth on it. Nothing accomplished. But . . . The other crows notice how much fun their friend is having and join in, taking turns swinging on the branch. Psychologist Anthony Pellegrini and others have concluded that play, in animals as well as humans, allows individuals to focus on means rather than ends. In play, an individual can try out new things, revise, modify, explore. Pass time pleasantly and, in subtle ways, develop the inner self. These researchers argue that the non-goal-oriented activities we call play have been a critical part of the development of problem-solving skills and emotional awareness in animals with more advanced cognitive abilities.

Pellegrini, who is also an educator, argues for more recess time in American schools. He notes that in most East Asian primary schools, for example, children are given a ten-minute break every forty minutes or so; in middle school they receive a ten-minute break every forty-five minutes; and in high school a ten-minute break every fifty minutes. According to various studies, when children come back from these breaks, they are more relaxed, more attentive, and more productive. Pellegrini notes that the trend in America has been a decrease in recess time.

My MIT colleague Woodie Flowers found a wonderful way to bring play into the classroom. Way back in the early

1970s, while a grad student, Flowers created a course at MIT called Introduction to Design. A central element of that course, which continues to this day, is to divide the students into teams and ask the teams to build a machine or robot that can accomplish a designated task. Over the years, the tasks have been such things as putting a round peg in a square hole; picking up a bunch of small items one at a time and carrying them from A to B; climbing up a steep ramp, and so on. Each team is given a box of identical supplies to work with: cardboard tubes, metal strips and cages, cords, motors, sprockets, rubber bands, wheels, gears and linkages, wires and batteries, diodes, silicon chips (in the later years), and photocells. The students have a few months to build their machines. At the end of the semester, there's a grand competition.

Flowers is emeritus now and no longer teaches this course. But during the years that he did, he would stage the competition event in a large lecture hall, with a hundred hollering and hooting MIT students gathered with their odd-looking contraptions. Then Flowers' gleeful announcement: "Let the best robot win." Even though all teams have been given the same task, the machines they come up with are wildly different. Imaginations have been unleashed. One group of students described the competition in this way: "We worked hard, toiling late into the night, hunched over our benches, twiddling, tweaking, refining, and all the other things we sophomore mechanical engineers do. And when the sawdust cleared, and the glue guns were cooled, we had 200 working machines ready for a contest." But these competitions and the months leading up to them are not work. They are sheer play, albeit with a goal in mind. Certainly, the students have been given some training in mechanical advantage, torque, and circuit boards, but they have also been given the time and space to play with that training. And while the competitions may appear to take place within the concrete walls of an established institution, they are actually unfolding in the infinite and unfettered minds of the students. Flowers has found a way to liberate the minds of these kids. He has given them permission to play. And watching them, I am reminded of my own "twiddling and tweaking" in my childhood lab. When I would hold a flame to the bimetal strip of a thermostat just to see what would happen.

5 The Free-Grazing Mind

Decades ago, when I was a graduate student in physics at the California Institute of Technology, I frequently saw a fellow grad student named Paul Schechter sitting on a certain bench between two buildings. Caltech, although small, was not a sleepy institution. It churned with adrenaline. But while other grad students were feverishly cranking out equations or soldering transistors in the lab, Paul sat quietly on his bench for hours, seemingly daydreaming. Recalling those years, Paul recently told me: "At Caltech, every time one of the professors walked by and saw me sitting on the bench, he would get a look of disapproval on his face, as if thinking 'grad students are supposed to look harried.' My best ideas came while I was sitting on that bench." In fact, during those years Schechter made a number of important cosmological discoveries, including a formula for the number of galaxies with different luminosities. Schechter, for many years now a professor at MIT, still sits on benches. "I sit on benches to clear my head," he says. "The benches overlooking the Charles [River] across from Building 14 were fantastic but they ripped them out ten years ago and never replaced them. The benches outside Stata aren't bad. The benches in JFK Park over by the Charles Hotel are pretty good."

In 1934, reporters at *The New Yorker* described the daily routine of author Gertrude Stein:

> Miss Stein gets up every morning about ten and drinks some coffee, against her will. She's always been nervous about becoming nervous and she thought coffee would make her nervous, but her doctor prescribed it. . . .
>
> Miss Stein has an outsize bathtub that was especially made for her. A staircase had to be taken out to install it. After her bath she puts on a huge wool bathrobe and writes for a while, but she prefers to write outdoors, after she gets dressed. Especially in the Ain country, because there are rocks and cows there. Miss Stein likes to look at rocks and cows in the intervals of her writing. The two ladies [Stein and her life partner, Alice B. Toklas] drive around in their Ford till they come to a good spot. Then Miss Stein gets out and sits on a campstool with pencil and pad, and Miss Toklas fearlessly switches a cow into her line of vision. If the cow doesn't seem to fit in with Miss Stein's mood, the ladies get into the car and drive on to another cow. When the great lady has an inspiration, she writes quickly, for about fifteen minutes. But often she just sits there, looking at cows and not turning a wheel.

Nobel Prize–winning pharmacologist Otto Loewi described the creative process of his most important discovery as follows:

The night before Easter Sunday of [1921] I awoke, turned on the light and jotted down a few notes on a tiny slip of thin paper. Then I fell asleep again. It occurred to me at six o'clock in the morning that during the night I had written down something important, but I was unable to decipher the scrawl. The next night, at three o'clock, the idea returned. It was the design of an experiment to determine whether or not the hypothesis of chemical transmission [of the nervous impulse from nerves to their respective organs] that I had uttered seventeen years ago was correct. I got up immediately, went to the laboratory, and performed a simple experiment on a frog heart according to the nocturnal design. . . . [A]n idea may sleep for decades in the unconscious mind and then suddenly return.

Filmmaker Federico Fellini described his morning routine in this way: "I'm up at six in the morning. I walk around the house, open windows, poke around boxes, move books from here to there. For years I've been trying to make myself a decent cup of coffee, but it's not one of my specialties. I go downstairs, outside as soon as possible." Evidently, Fellini rambled around in order to give free rein to his artistic imagination.

The great mathematician Henri Poincaré wrote this about one of his important discoveries:

For fifteen days, I strove to prove that there could not be any [mathematical] functions like those I have since called Fuchsian functions. I was then very ignorant; every day I seated

myself at my work table, stayed an hour or two, tried a great
number of combinations and reached no results. One evening,
contrary to my custom, I drank black coffee and could not
sleep. Ideas rose in crowds; I felt them collide until pairs interlocked, so to speak, making a stable combination. By the next
morning I had established the existence of a class of Fuchsian
functions . . .

If we try to understand these various creative processes
in terms of the workings of the brain, it seems evident that
something must be going on at the unconscious level, or at
least the relaxed level. For centuries, scientists thought that
the brain must be quiet during periods of rest, when people
are sleeping or relaxing or not consciously engaged in a
purposeful activity. That view was dramatically changed in
the 1920s by a German psychiatrist and physicist named Hans
Berger. Berger single-handedly invented the electroenceph-
alogram (EEG), what he called the *Elektrenkephalogramm*.
He sometimes referred to his invention as a "brain mirror."
By inserting silver wires under his patients' scalps, one at the
front of the head and one at the back, and hooking the wires
to a galvanometer, he could measure the electrical activity
of the brain. Later, he could see distinct patterns of electrical
waveforms that changed with the psychological state of his
subjects. What Berger found, among other things, was that
the brain is *always* busy, even during periods of apparent rest.

In fact, the brain uses only about five percent less energy when at rest than when consciously at work.

Berger's path to his invention is a remarkable story. He dropped out of university and enlisted in the military. Then, one spring morning in 1892, the nineteen-year-old Berger had an experience that changed his life and the history of science. He was riding a horse and pulling behind him a piece of heavy artillery. Suddenly, his horse bucked and threw Berger to the ground. The artillery gun kept rolling and stopped just at the last moment before it would have crushed the young man. That night, Berger received a telegram from his father, the first telegram he'd ever received from his family. The message expressed concern for his health. It turned out that young Berger's older sister had felt a strong sense of danger that day and had urged their father to contact her brother. Shaken and amazed, Berger was not able to explain the extraordinary events in terms of known science, or coincidence. He concluded that his feelings of imminent death during those few seconds must have taken some physical form, traveled through space, and been received by his sister several hundred miles away. After the near-death experience, Berger went back to university, changed majors to medicine, and determined to spend the rest of his life understanding the nature of "psychic energy."

Although Berger never found what could be called psychic energy, his invention of the EEG machine and discovery of the continuous activity of the brain have been of major importance. In the 1950s, other researchers found that the metabolism and energy needs of the brain remained the same during resting and non-resting states. Beginning in the 1990s, neuroscientist and psychiatrist Nancy Andreasen at the University of Iowa Hospitals and Clinics and her collaborators, and neurologist Marcus Raichle at Washington University and his collaborators, used positron emission tomography (PET) to do more detailed studies of brain activity during resting and non-resting states. Andreasen invented the term "REST" (random episodic silent thinking) for the high degree of brain activity during resting states, while Raichle coined the term "default mode" for the same activity.

Andreasen and her colleagues have been particularly interested in the kind of mental wandering commonly called free association. She has found that when subjects are engaged in free-floating thoughts, a particular part of the brain called the association cortex is highly active. Furthermore, at these moments other parts of the brain associated with more directed and task-specific activities are relatively quiet. And vice versa. In other words, researchers have shown both that the brain is busy all of the time and that some regions are more active during directed and goal-oriented thinking while others are more active during "restful" or free-floating periods. Evidently, there is a material, neural basis for directed versus undirected thought. It seems only a short additional step to hypothesize that some of the human creative process takes place when the brain is in default mode and in the associated regions. Something physically identifiable goes on when we let our minds wander and spin.

What is creativity? And how is it connected to free association, to letting the mind wander and spin? Despite all the research by neuroscientists and psychologists, creativity remains largely a mystery (and happily so, in my opinion). The great American writer E. B. White described his writing process this way: "[T]he truth is I write by ear, always with difficulty and seldom with any exact notion of what is taking place under the hood." Nevertheless, there is a little we do know about creativity. First of all, and perhaps surprisingly, it is not closely connected to intelligence. For several decades, beginning in 1921, the psychologist Lewis Terman followed the lives of 1,500 people with high IQs, in the range of 135 to 200. Although this cohort of people had more success in their lives and careers than the average person, they were not found to be unusually creative. In conjunction with Terman's findings, other studies have shown that highly creative people have average IQs, around 120.

Theories of creativity abound. Freud and Jung believed that people become creative in reaction to difficulties or repressed emotions. "Unsatisfied wishes are the driving power behind fantasies," wrote Freud, and fantasies lead to creative ideas. Another theory is that creativity is associated with mild mental illness. People are more creative when they are more self-reflective, and self-reflection is sometimes associated with depression. Fear of death may motivate some people to create, to produce something immortal. The psychologist Abraham Maslow argued for several different kinds of creativity. Primary creativity involves an escape from the stress of the day. When we paint or write or make music, we usually leave our stresses behind. Another of Maslow's creativities is what he calls "self-actualization," the desire to become the best we can be—personal growth at the highest level. Clearly, some kinds of creativity, especially the more intellectual, are associated with curiosity about the world (Einstein), or the desire to express one's individuality and vision (Picasso). Still, these are only theories. Undoubtedly, there are different kinds of creativity.

On one aspect of creativity most researchers agree. It is something called "divergent thinking": the ability to explore many different avenues and solutions to a problem in a spontaneous and non-orderly fashion. "Convergent thinking," by contrast, is the more logical and orderly step-by-step approach to a problem. Divergent thinking is more free-flowing than convergent thinking. Recall Poincaré's description of his creative process: "Ideas rose in crowds; I felt them collide until pairs interlocked, so to speak, making a stable combination."

Divergent thinking does not cooperate on demand. It is not easily summoned. It does not follow the clock. It cannot be rushed. It withers and fades under external schedules and noise and assignments. Rather, it lollygags along on its own;

it sprawls in the sun, taking its own time. Divergent thinking is associated with play, creativity, and curiosity. The psychologist J. Nina Lieberman and others have found, not surprisingly, a correlation between the spontaneous play of children and the intellectual activity of adults engaged in divergent thinking.

Some years ago, I was working on a novel and was profoundly stuck. The main character David, a man in his midforties, had started suffering from unexplained physical and mental illnesses and was gradually becoming dysfunctional. It was his wife, Melissa, I didn't understand. She had grown up poor, attained some degree of prosperity and security upon marrying David, but now was afraid that she would lose everything with David's disintegration. After finding some comfort in an online affair, she turned to alcohol. Then she began treating David with contempt and complete lack of sympathy. The more miserable and pathetic her husband, the harsher she became. At least, that is how I imagined her in my early drafts. But I could not bring her to life. Her actions and dialogue were stiff and wooden. I thought I knew her, but every scene with her was a disaster, a painting with a patch of canvas ripped out of it. Over a period of several years, my novel had gone through multiple drafts but remained paralyzed by the problem of Melissa. One day as I was taking a shower, I suddenly had an insight about Melissa: she was doing the best she could. There was one piece of new dialogue—I think a single sentence—that suddenly came to me and revealed this vital aspect of her character. After that, she

became flesh and blood. At the time, it seemed I had acciden-
tally stumbled upon those few telling words out of her mouth.
But in retrospect, I realize that my mind had been imagining
a large range of possible Melissas, each responding to her
husband's illness in a different way. Some of this imagining
surely happened unconsciously. Each different Melissa was a
new invention. And each different Melissa, in my free-flowing
explorations, had uttered different words at that critical
point in the story. Perhaps unconsciously, I was testing out
different Melissas. Eventually, one of those trial-and-error
sentences had pulled along with it a Melissa who rang true to
me. Not only that but a Melissa I could feel for, and even love,
despite the despicable way she treated her desperate husband.
Because I realized that she was desperate, too. Given her
earlier history, she was doing the best she could. I know that I
did not come upon this understanding by any logical or linear
path. It was, I think, divergent thinking.

I had a similar experience when I was stuck on a physics
problem in graduate school. I was trying to prove or disprove
a certain proposition about the nature of gravity, conjectured
some years earlier by a Stanford physicist. I had written down
all the equations to be solved, but a known partial result at
the halfway point was not coming out right. I knew I had to
be making a mistake, but I could not find my mistake. For
several months, I had been going over and over my equations
without success. Then one morning I woke up with a new
idea, a realization of something I had not taken into account.

I had not quite dreamed the idea, as Otto Loewi did, but it had definitely appeared in my head at first light, just after a night's sleep, when I was totally relaxed and not consciously thinking about anything. I was certainly not directing my conscious awareness toward the problem that had been stumping me for months. Excited, I went to my desk, got out my twenty coffee-stained pages of calculations, and found where I had made my error. In hours, I proved that the proposition was true.

None of this is to say that creativity is never associated with convergent thinking. A great deal of creative work in mathematics and science involves a focused and conscious effort to solve well-posed problems with unique and definite solutions. Much of this work involves directed and orderly thinking. In his search for an equation describing the subatomic particle called the electron, physicist Paul Dirac knew that he must follow a narrow path fenced in by Einstein's relativity and the new quantum physics of Schrödinger and Heisenberg. Likewise, when Hans Krebs discovered the sequence of chemical steps by which energy is released by the ingestion of food, he purposefully looked for a particular and unique part of the sequence that would complete a *cycle* of reactions, returning the intermediate molecules to the same starting point. It is hard to know what role the unconscious mind plays in such discoveries, but certainly the conscious effort is logical and orderly.

It is possible that both unconscious and conscious thought are required in certain kinds of discovery. Both spontaneous

and deliberated considerations. Both non-orderly and orderly mental investigations. I would argue, however, that in most and perhaps all forms of creative activity, an unencumbered, unregimented, inward-looking mind is required at certain points—a mind that has unplugged from the wired world.

In 1926, the British social psychologist and educator Graham Wallas proposed that creative thinking follows a series of stages: preparation, incubation, illumination, and finally verification. In the preparation stage, the person does his or her homework or research in a field or art form or any other endeavor, masters the tools of the craft, and defines some problem. In the incubation stage, the person mulls over the problem in various ways, sometimes unconsciously. In the illumination stage, the person achieves a new insight or shift of perspective. And in the verification stage, the person puts the insight to the test and works out the consequences. I suggest that "divergent thinking" occurs in the incubation and illumination stages, between which there is no sharp boundary. The incubation and illumination stages seem to require a relaxed mind, not actively pounding away at the project. In those stages, the mind wanders in the default mode. But still burns up calories. T. S. Eliot had this to say about the incubation stage in his craft:

> [T]he material has obviously been incubating within the poet, and cannot be suspected of being in present form a friendly or impertinent demon. What one writes in this way may succeed

in standing the examination of a more normal state of mind; it gives me the impression, as I have said, of having undergone a long incubation, though we do not know until the shell breaks what kind of egg we have been sitting on.

And Alexander Graham Bell celebrated unconscious thought with these words:

I am a believer in unconscious cerebration. The brain is working all the time, though we do not know it. At night, it follows up what we think in the daytime. When I have worked a long time on one thing, I make it a point to bring all the facts regarding it together before I retire; and I have often been surprised at the results.

Some years ago, I did a study of great scientific discoveries of the twentieth century. The discovery of the first hormone by William Bayliss and Ernest Starling in 1902; the discovery of relativity by Albert Einstein in 1905; the discovery of a method to measure the distance to the stars by Henrietta Leavitt in 1912; the discovery of the universal chemical reactions in energy production in living cells by Hans Krebs in 1937; the discovery of the structure of DNA by Rosalind Franklin, James Watson, and Francis Crick in 1953; and so on. There were two dozen in all. Among other things, I was interested to see if there were any common patterns of discovery. And what I found was that many of the discoveries followed the stages of

(1) preparation, (2) being stuck, (3) new insight or change of perspective, and finally, (4) discovery. At the time, I was not aware of the work of Wallas. In retrospect, I believe that my second stage, being stuck, might have some of the qualities of Wallas's incubation period. The "stuckness" itself, the impasse, is important. Being stuck catalyzes the creative imagination. When we are stuck on a problem, our mind roams through a vast terrain of possible solutions—just as I did when trying to understand the character of Melissa. Lise Meitner was stuck on understanding how a single diminutive neutron could split apart a giant uranium nucleus, until she realized that the atomic nucleus might be unstable when slightly deformed, as when a drop of water, when stretched, splits in two. Barbara McClintock was stuck on figuring out how genes can turn on and off during the lifetime of a single organism, until she realized that genetic elements might be transferred from one sister chromatid to another in the cell division process.

I believe that getting stuck is often an essential part of the creative process. And when we are stuck—if we have managed to escape the heave and rush of the world, if we have managed to secure solitude and quiet and space without time—then our minds can roam and explore and invent in unfettered freedom. But too often we dread being stuck. Especially our students and young people. We believe that if we are stuck we have failed. On the contrary, we should welcome getting stuck. We should embrace getting stuck. That's when discovery begins. If we have a prepared mind, if we have done our homework, then getting stuck is a trumpet call to our creative imaginations. I might add here that having a prepared mind is essential to the creative process. To my knowledge, none of the great scientific discoveries of the twentieth century—and certainly none in my own study—were made by amateurs. In all cases, the scientists had done their homework and had mastered the tools of their trade. Their minds had been fertilized. And then they got stuck.

Which brings us back once again to the unhappy teen on the cover of *Time*. She is trapped in the grid. She is trapped in the hyperconnected and time-driven world of today. She has difficulty being alone within her own mind because she has become addicted to constant external stimulation. She is not able to give herself the quiet and the privacy to let her mind wander, to explore new terrain. Above all else, she has not developed the *habit of mind* for contemplation and reflection. The hyperconnected Internet of today certainly has not encouraged that needed habit of mind. Gertrude Stein and Otto Loewi and Federico Fellini had no trouble contemplating or spending time by themselves. But one does not have to be a creative genius to develop this habit of mind. One needs only the desire and willpower to unplug from the grid, to separate from the rush and the heave. It is the nurturing of one's inner spirit, that whispering voice. It is the celebration of privacy and solitude. It is the willingness to follow one's own thoughts. It is the indulgence of play and unscheduled time.

My wife is a painter. She spent ten years as an apprentice in the atelier of a master painter in Boston. There, she learned the craft of painting in the classical tradition, how to defocus her eyes and see only the unshaped lights and shadows of a scene, how to turn the rounded form of a vase, how to lose edges, how to set up a still life. After a decade of such training, she struck out on her own and got her own studio, a room in a converted school building with large north-facing windows for good light. Every day, she goes there for hours, alone, and creates. I've had the good fortune in my life to mingle with many of her fellow painters as well as my own scientific and literary colleagues. I've also known musical composers. One thing all these people share is an embrace of solitude. Not that these are unsociable people. But they practice their craft in solitude. They draw strength from being alone while they create or explore new worlds. They need that aloneness. They have developed the habit of mind to accept and seek out that aloneness. Sometimes, they must push back against their society to get what they need.

One of the most disturbing effects of the wired world is its impact on the creativity of young people. Researcher Kyung Hee Kim of the School of Education at William and Mary, in a much-noted article titled "The Creativity Crisis: The Decrease in Creative Thinking Scores on the Torrance Tests of Creative Thinking," has concluded that creativity has decreased among all Americans since 1990, and that the decrease has been most severe for kindergartners through third graders. In her study, Dr. Kim analyzed the results over time of the Torrance Tests of Creative Thinking, which was first developed in 1966 and has been taken by more than 270,000 kindergartners through adults from 1966 to 2008. Some representative tasks on the Torrance tests are: take a list of common objects and suggest ways to improve those objects; write an interesting and exciting story after a prompt; given the drawings of ten stimulus figures on a piece of paper, design novel objects by adding lines to the figures; given the shape of a triangle or a jelly bean, think of a picture in which that shape appears. Kim found that since 1990 there has been a significant decrease in children's ability to produce unique and unusual ideas and to think in a detailed and reflective manner. Summarizing her results, she writes that since 1990, "[C]hildren have become less emotionally expressive, less energetic, less talkative and verbally expressive, less humorous, less imaginative, less unconventional, less lively and passionate, less perceptive, less apt to connect seemingly irrelevant things, less synthesizing, and less likely to see things from a different angle."

The date 1990 approximately coincides with the public emergence of the Internet, the rapid increase in speed of communication, and a general increase in the pace of life in general. I would argue that the wired world is clearly the culprit in the loss of creativity found by Dr. Kim and other researchers. In a world that is hurried and time-driven, overscheduled, noisy, hyperconnected, and wired twenty-four/seven, we have less time for play, for quiet reflection, for free grazing of the imagination, for thinking and absorbing what we have learned, for invention. There is little time to waste, even for children.

Although divergent thinking and invention may dwell in the shadows of the unconscious and the unscheduled, I believe they can be brought into the light. I believe that divergent thinking can be cultivated. Partly, it is a matter of habit of mind. Partly, it is a matter of unplugging. Sometimes, when I am searching for an idea or literary reference or even a single word—the right word—I can feel my mind lift off and begin wandering. I trust that inward experience. I might be looking out the window of a moving train, watching the trees go by. And then I can no longer see the trees. I have disappeared into that magical place of my mind. I am both aware and unaware. I am flesh and not flesh. I am unleashed from time. I am free.

6 Downtime and Replenishment

A few years ago, I went to a ten-day Tibetan Buddhist retreat in a lovely rural area of Wisconsin. My wife was well practiced in Buddhist meditation and, for many years, had set aside twenty minutes a day for the activity. I had been trying it out now and then. Finally, I decided to give myself over to the experience at a bona fide retreat center. So I carved out a chunk from my schedule and headed for Wisconsin.

Each day, we participants sat through seven or eight hours of guided meditation, broken up by meals. For the rest of the time, we read, took long walks, and just abided alone with our thoughts. There was little else to do. The center had not orchestrated other activities. I don't recall seeing any laptops or smartphones. None of us attempted to contact our workplaces or glance at our to-do lists. The meditation center itself was sprawled out in the middle of nowhere—surrounded by miles of farmland punctuated only by the occasional wood farmhouse and a few wandering cows.

Meditation is a beautiful and profound experience. While meditating, you quiet your mind as much as possible. You focus on the moment. When random thoughts arise, as they invariably do, you learn not to dwell on them but simply to acknowledge them and let them go, like momentary ripples on a lake. Needless to say, while meditating you are off the grid. You are free from the stimulation of the external world. You have dedicated a few minutes to stillness of mind.

Although the methodology has not always been of uniform quality, numerous studies have suggested the physical and psychological benefits of meditation. To mention only one recent study, psychologists Ruth Baer, Emily Lykins, and Jessica Peters at the University of Kentucky and Eastern Kentucky University reported that the "psychological wellbeing" of seventy-seven regular meditators was significantly better than that of seventy-five non-meditators. Psychological well-being was measured on a scale with six elements: self-acceptance, positive relations with others, autonomy, environmental mastery, purpose in life, and personal growth. Biologist and leading meditation researcher Jon Kabat-Zinn and his collaborators have observed physical alterations in the brain produced by mindfulness meditation.

I found the meditation sessions to be restful, interesting, and valuable as a tool for reducing stress. But meditation is only one way of distancing yourself from the rush and heave of the world. Whatever psychological benefit I received from meditating during my ten days in Wisconsin, I derived an equal benefit from the quiet time outside the meditation room. Downtime. My mind was unleashed. And instead of trying to empty my mind, as one does in meditation, and letting my thoughts drift by like moving clouds, I followed my thoughts, but in an unhurried and liberated way. Without setting out to do so, I began sewing together the pieces of my life. I found myself recalling people and places of the past, conversations, words said and unsaid, deeds I was proud of and others I regretted. I remembered the particular moment when I made my maiden voyage on a two-wheeler—a wobbly trip across the front yard, dodging trees—while my father looked on with pride and support. I remembered taking walks with my mother in her last months of life, she wearing a silly feathered hat to cover her newly bald head. Her words to me: "Life is too short to spend time with people you don't enjoy being with." I recalled my silent resolution to try to live life so that when my own last moments arrived I would be at peace. I remembered a high school friend who had abruptly stopped answering my letters and phone calls when we reached our forties. With some sleuthing, I confirmed that he was alive and well. I recalled my hurt and my soul-searching for how I might have wounded him, and the final letter I wrote to him apologizing for all that might have gone wrong. Who was I in those blossoming years? Had I misunderstood myself? I played mental movies of my life in other decades, seeing myself outside of myself like a character on a stage. I remembered sounds and scenes, shuffled in time like cards in a deck: standing with a girlfriend in an abandoned railway car in the middle of a grassy field; a grotesque chandelier I'd bought on a whim to hang in my first apartment in Pasadena; Paul

McCartney singing "Yesterday"; demonstrating a prism to my ten-year-old daughter by holding it up to a window and pointing to the splash of colors cast on the wall; a thick book lying half open on a table. Large things and small. I found myself mulling over the principles I believed in, other principles I once believed in but had abandoned, what I wanted to do with the rest of my life. My children. My wife.

There was no hurry in these recollections and daydreams. There was no urgency. All these thoughts emerged in a quiet and leisurely manner, like a bubble of air slowly rising to the surface in a still summer pond.

Here are a few sections I wrote in my journal at the time:

> I think there are several different goals that motivate people to action:

1. the pure joy of helping others, without expecting anything in return
2. the belief in certain values that require action
3. the desire to have an impact in the world, to make a difference; one can further desire personal credit for having an impact, in which case the ego is involved, or one can seek an impact without any desire to receive personal credit
4. the desire to promote one's self or achieve personal gain, regardless of whether there is any positive impact on the world

A big issue for me is dealing with disappointments when one of my projects does not have the consequence I hoped for.

For me the big questions about life are:

1.   How should I live in the world?
2.   Why should I live this way?

One answer to both is that I should live so as to bring myself satisfaction. Satisfaction in and of itself is a worthy goal, because we have only one life (in my opinion), and we might as well be personally satisfied in that one life.

I have wonderful memories of my grandparents, parents, aunts and uncles, brothers and cousins, at large family gatherings at my grandparents' house. These gatherings made me feel warm, safe, protected, in the "bosom of the family."

What were these musings about? I think they were about the renewal and consolidation of my identity. My time wandering alone in the fields around the retreat center or reading quietly in a vacant chair connected me to myself. I felt that I was revisiting myself, perhaps even revising myself. I felt that I was walking through the rooms of my life and having conversations with all the people I had met there. In those rooms, I met younger versions of myself as well. They were all me, of course, in my childhood and teens and twenties and thirties and on. I could understand them and acknowledge them. I could acknowledge the union of my selves. I could see the center. I felt a deep completeness; my various selves united as one self, sometimes making good decisions, sometimes not good, but always trying to live well in the world, trying to be part of a whole. I could see the fullness of my life, and the aspirations. And the rooms of the future were there as well, with doors slightly ajar, offering glimpses of what I might become in the world ahead of me, the world I could control and the world I could not. I heard the quiet, whispering voice saying, "This is who I am. This is who I want to be. This is my cosmos of being." In one of her poems, Emily Dickinson compared stillness to a smooth mind. Stillness is what I felt. And my mind was rounding.

Mental downtime is having the space and freedom to wander about the vast hallways of memory and contemplate who we are. Downtime is when we can ponder our past and imagine our future. Downtime is when we can repair our selves. Such renewal differs in some ways from the creative activity discussed in the last chapter. But both require unplugging from the grid. And you don't have to go to a meditation center in rural Wisconsin to unplug. All you need is time away from the rush and heave of the world. Quiet time. Alone time. And you need a certain habit of mind. You need a regular pattern of thinking and approaching life, a deeply rooted and constant manner of honoring your inner self, affirming your values, and arranging your life so as to live by those values.

In the business world, the technology world, and the computer world, "downtime" is a dirty word. It means a period when the system is not working, when the computers have crashed, when the machines have temporarily ground to a halt. In these contexts, downtime is considered useless time, empty time. But for the lush and mysterious terrain of our minds, downtime is a chance to explore. It is a time to renew. It is also a chance to restore and maintain our equilibrium.

One of the definitions of a living organism, at a primitive level, involves the ability to separate itself from its surroundings and create a stable and orderly environment within itself. That stable equilibrium is called homeostasis. An organism receives outside stimulation—indeed, it must receive, at a minimum, energy from the exterior world—but it needs to regulate that stimulation and maintain a coherent and stable interior. The organism separates itself from the outer world with some kind of outer membrane. It lets certain materials inside itself through that membrane but not others. And it expels some materials through that membrane. Through all these processes, the organism must remain whole. The organism cannot dissolve. It cannot merge with its surroundings. Its interior parts must understand what they are supposed to do (at least at the biochemical level) and proceed with their designated activities.

Homeostasis can happen at the mindless level of an amoeba. Or at the more advanced level of a human being. And at that more advanced level, I suggest that there is a kind of necessary homeostasis of the mind: not a static equilibrium but a dynamic equilibrium in which we are constantly examining, testing, and replenishing our mental system, constantly securing the mental membrane between ourselves and the external world, constantly reorganizing and affirming ourselves. Dynamic rather than static because the outside world is constantly changing, and we ourselves are constantly changed by it. And yet we must maintain an equilibrium in the face of change. We cannot disintegrate. We cannot succumb to the random noise of the world. We must constantly examine who we are, revise when revision is needed, and bring coherency to all the parts of our whole.

Downtime enables not only our creativity and our need for rest. It also enables the formation and maintenance of our deep sense of being and identity. The great Swiss psychiatrist Carl Jung discussed identity in terms of the Self, which he pictured as a circle. For Jung, the Self was the result of integrating one's life experiences into a whole—but a whole distinct from its surroundings, as in the biological understanding of homeostasis.

The need to nourish the Self, the need for some kind of equilibrium and homeostasis within ourselves and our immediate environment, must be buried deep in our psyche, going back to our most primitive origins. Yet in the hyperconnected, overstimulated, and time-driven world of today, we are often far from equilibrium. We often lack the time and space for personal reflection. We lack the mental quiet and privacy to create a necessary inner stability.

I would suggest that the absence of downtime works on our bodies and minds in the same way as does sleep deprivation. One of the first experimental studies of sleep deprivation was done by the Russian physician and scientist Maria Mikhailovna Manaseina. In 1894, Manaseina reported that young dogs deprived of sleep died within a few days. Her experiments were repeated a few years later with older dogs by the Italian physiologists Lamberto Daddi and Giulio Tarozzi, with the same results. These researchers were not able to attribute the cause of death to lack of food or physical exhaustion. Even today, the function of sleep is not fully understood. But many scientists feel that the quiet of sleep, without external stimulation and stress, is needed to rejuvenate mental processes as well as to repair muscles and tissues. Sleep is an opportunity for the mind, freed from the noise of the waking world, to take stock. Such accounting is critically important to organize the zillions of sensory and mental experiences that bombard us each day.

Without downtime, we might not physically die, but we will die psychologically, emotionally, spiritually. In downtime, not only are we making sense of the events of the day, we are making sense of our lives. We are combing through the thousands of hours and days of our lives to find those

experiences and thoughts that have personal meaning to us, that speak to us, sometimes in that quiet, whispering voice.

One of the memories that keeps coming back to me when I have downtime is a moment when I was twelve years old, away at summer camp. I was small for my age, and socially awkward to boot. Consequently, I suffered a fair amount of derision and ridicule from the other boys at the camp. The moment that recurs in my thoughts happened during a particular baseball game. Among boys at that age, athletic prowess is prized above all else, and I was not a particularly strong athlete. Nevertheless, the coach of my team, a counselor in his late twenties who always wore a Yankees hat, had been encouraging me all summer. When it was my time to bat in that particular game, I was frightened that I would strike out, a further confirmation of my ineptitude and worthlessness. Anxiously, I stepped up to the plate. The first pitch was a fastball. I swung with all my might. Miraculously, I hit the ball right at the sweet spot of the bat. *Crack!* The ball exploded from my bat and shot over the head of the most distant outfielder. I still remember the moment like it was yesterday. I can still hear the sharp crack when the ball met the bat. I can still feel the vibration of the bat in my hands. But what I remember most was the feeling of power. I had never felt that power before. That was the beginning of my life as a person of power, and I continue to draw from that one moment in all my endeavors, especially when I am embarking on an uncertain and difficult task. I remind myself that I am a person of power. Somewhere in my psyche, in the vaporous regions of memory and Self and shape-shifting meaning, a twelve-year-old boy stands at the plate and wallops the ball. I hope that I will always have moments of quiet to feel and touch him.

7 Chronos and Kairos

Over the years, I've made many trips to Tramung Chrum, and I've become friends with the villagers. Despite the language and cultural differences, we've exchanged meaningful words. We've laughed together, shared meals together, sat together at celebrations and funerals. My older daughter has slept overnight in the village and been treated as one of their children. And I've learned that the villagers' concept of time— exemplified by the woman who never considered how long it took to go to the market—is fundamental to their way of being in the world. They live in a world not of time but of space. And that very fact creates more space, creates *spaciousness*, not only in their sprawling rice fields but also in their minds. Reflection, contemplation, examination, free-floating thoughts and ideas naturally bloom in that space. For the villagers of Tramung Chrum, time is a different substance than it is for me. Some of the villagers own wristwatches, but they are almost ornamental. The day's physical and mental rhythms are marked by events, not by the minutes and hours registered on mechanical and digital clocks.

My experience with this remote village on the other side of the planet reminds me of the two different words for time in ancient Greece: *chronos* and *kairos*. *Chronos* is clock time. (And the ancient Greeks did have crude clocks, called water clocks, in which time was measured by the flow of water.) *Chronos* is quantitative time. *Chronos* is sequential time. *Chronos* is the relentless time that marches on mindlessly in the external world, oblivious to the lives of human beings. *Kairos*, on the other hand, is time created by events, often human events. It might be the opportune moment to take action. *Kairos* is not necessarily measurable in minutes and hours. It might be the duration of a season, or of a meal, or of a love affair. When an event of human significance occurs, it occupies a great deal of *kairos*. When insignificant, its *kairos* might be nothing at all. *Kairos* time is forever. It is the time of memory. It is the time of being.

The ancient Romans also distinguished between two different kinds of time: *negotium* and *otium*. *Negotium* was time spent at work and duty. Business time. *Otium* was leisure time, time spent away from the job. *Otium* was time for reflection, reading, writing, thinking, philosophizing, self-examination. Cicero, during the periods when he was between official jobs, ousted from public duty, used his *otium* to write books of philosophy.

As I discovered in Tramung Chrum, our relationship to time and its uses can vary from culture to culture. While modern communication technologies have undoubtedly hastened the pace of life and reduced the time available for quiet reflection, other cultural and even geographical factors can also alter the conception of time. Tejinder Billing, an associate professor of management and entrepreneurship at Rowan University in New Jersey who studies attitudes toward time, recently told me that when she teaches a class that ends at ten thirty, her students begin looking at their watches or smartphones at ten twenty. "I realized that people [in the United States] are so driven by the clock," she said. "I actually didn't find one single room in my school that didn't have a clock. In India [where I grew up] clocks are not of such importance . . . In India, time is like the flow of a river. We just stay in the moment. Time is abundant. It is not like money. It is not going to go away."

In research on time use in fourteen countries, Billing and her collaborators reported that Westerners—and especially Westerners in the more developed countries—view time as linear, measured by clocks, whereas non-Westerners view time as nonlinear, as a measure of the interpersonal, social, and cultural significance of events. *Chronos* and *kairos*. In countries like the United States, Canada, the United Kingdom, and Germany, time is a precious resource, not to be wasted. By contrast, in countries like Mexico and India, and various countries in Latin America, "it is common to accept with indifference that what does not get done today will get done tomorrow, and that appointments are mere approximations."

Robert Levine, a professor of psychology at California State University (Fresno), has studied the pace of life in countries all over the world and describes his results in a fascinating book titled *A Geography of Time*. In each country, Levine and his collaborators used three different measures of the pace of life: average walking speed, the time taken for a postal clerk to fulfill a request for stamps, and the accuracy of clocks at fifteen randomly selected banks. Levine and others have determined several principal factors that are associated with the tempo of life: economic well-being, the degree of industrialization, population size, climate, and the degree of individualism versus collectivism in the culture.

Economic well-being is the single-largest determinant of the pace of life. The fastest living is found in the wealthier countries such as those in North America, Northern Europe, and some Asian nations such as Japan and Korea. The slowest is in less economically prosperous countries such as those in Central and South America, most countries in the Middle East, and India. It is not surprising that economic well-being is correlated with a high speed of living. Modern communication technologies, which accelerate the pace of life, are more widespread in the wealthier nations. Most importantly, the time-equals-money equation is more prominent in the more productive and prosperous societies.

The degree of industrialization, of course, is closely related to economic well-being—and both drive a faster lifestyle. One of the great ironies of modern technology, pointed out by Levine and many others, is that the so-called labor-saving devices, such as vacuum cleaners and dishwashers, have not created more leisure time but the opposite. There are at least two explanations for this contradiction. Greater technical advances and devices have led to *greater expectations*. Since it is easier to keep the house clean, we demand a higher state of cleanliness. Higher expectations take more time. Secondly, greater efficiency in the workplace (produced by fax machines, scanners, computers, etc.) has also led to greater expectations. The last fifty years have shown that we do not put gains in productivity into taking more days off. Instead, we and our bosses expect greater output. In fact, the sociologist Juliet Schor, in her important book *The Overworked American*, found that the average American is actually working more hours per year than in the past. (Her studies covered the period 1970 to 1990.) All these findings are perfectly illustrated by my lawyer friend, mentioned earlier, who told me that with the advent of e-mail, her clients "want immediate turnaround, even on complex matters." With greater efficiency, we simply increase the workload, accelerating the pace of life.

For me, the most provocative of Levine's findings is the correlation between pace of life and degree of individualism in the culture. "Individualist" societies such as the United States are more likely to regard time as a precious resource. Individualist societies place more importance on achievement. And achievement within the industrial-techno-logical-commercial complex leads to the time-equals-money equation. As an American, when I consider my personal relationship to the world, I think of myself as an individual finding my place in "the system." I must make my personal mark on it. And that system is orchestrated by schedules and appointments. By contrast, "collectivist" societies, such as India and Mexico, where the emphasis is on the group and on social relationships, have a more relaxed attitude toward time. If a family is getting together for dinner, it is not so important that everyone arrive at the table at the same time or leave at the same time. An uncle is running a bit late because he misplaced his dentures. An aunt came a bit early because she wanted to help out in the kitchen. No matter. Hugs, food, conversation, long walks in the evening after the meal do not follow a schedule.

Attitudes about time regulate life, and the rhythms of life regulate attitudes about time. When the pace of life is faster, when we have greater expectations of achievement each hour and each day, we must necessarily make schedules. We must necessarily look at the clock. We must necessarily fit our lives into slots of time. When the clock says eight, we must leave for work, or else we will be late. When the clock says ten, we must appear at the ten o'clock meeting, or else the boss will decide we are wasting her time. When the clock says four, we must pick our child up from school so we can take him to his music

lesson at four thirty. In such a manner of living, time becomes a steel mesh, laid down by an all-powerful but invisible dictator each morning the moment we wake. (Oh, for those lovely moments of sleep at night when time doesn't exist!) The edges of that "time mesh" are cold and hard. Each day, we must cram ourselves and the events of our lives into it. Clocks, watches, digital devices are the guardians and lieutenants of the mesh. They are constantly shouting at us to keep in step, to mind the mesh.

Some years ago, I wrote a short novel about time called *Einstein's Dreams*. In the book, my fictional Einstein dreams about many different possibilities for the nature of time as he is slowly working his way toward his own theory of time, called relativity. In one of Einstein's dreamed worlds, there are two times: mechanical time and body time. The people who live by mechanical time rise at seven each morning, eat their lunch at noon, and their supper at six. They make love between eight and ten at night. "When their stomachs growl, they look at their watch to see if it is time to eat. When they begin to lose themselves in a concert, they look at the clock above the stage to see when it will be time to go home." The people who live by body time do not keep clocks. "Instead, they listen to their heartbeats. . . . Such people eat when they are hungry, go to their jobs at the millinery or the chemist's whenever they wake from their sleep, make love all hours of the day." In retrospect, I believe that I was writing about *chronos* and *kairos*, although I did not realize it. What I did understand, at least unconsciously, was the need for unscheduled time, the need for an inner life, the need for space without time.

Most of us in America and other developed countries are living by *chronos* time, even more rigid and impersonal than in the days of the ancient Greeks. In such a life, where are the moments to truly experience the world and ourselves? Where are the moments to absorb and reflect? Where are the moments to let our minds wander, free from the steel mesh of time? Where are the moments to *waste* time?

There may even be a religious component in our communion with time. Consider the United States and England. According to the deep Puritan ethic imported from England in the founding of America and still present today, it is actually a sin to waste time.

We can, perhaps, trace the roots of this ethic to the *Westminster Shorter Catechism*, written in 1646 and 1647 by the Westminster Assembly, a group of English and Scottish theologians. Most Puritans who colonized America in the seventeenth century subscribed to the *Catechism*. Question 61 reads: "What is forbidden in the fourth commandment?" The answer: "The fourth commandment forbiddeth the omission, or careless performance, of the duties required, and the profaning the day by idleness, or doing that which is in itself sinful, or by unnecessary thoughts, words, or works, about our worldly employments or recreations." Note that "idleness" is considered a profanity.

A highly influential proponent of the ideas in the *Westminster Shorter Catechism* was the Puritan theologian Richard Baxter (1615–1691), who himself was credited with authoring some 165 books. In a chapter of one of Baxter's books titled "How to Conquer Sloth and Idleness by the Life of Faith," we read: "The greater and more excellent any man's work and calling is, his idleness and negligence is the greater sin. . . . Christ biddeth us pray 'the Lord of the harvest to send forth labourers into his harvest;' (Luke x.27) and not proud, covetous, idle drones . . . The highest title that was ever put on pastors was to be 'Labourers together with God' (1 Cor. iii.9)."

I would argue that even today, four centuries later, we can find deep in the American consciousness the Puritan work ethic that wasting time is immoral, that wasting time is a sin against God. A contemporary religious website titled *Life of a Steward* claims that "Wasting time is a sin because even the tiniest misuse of time shows that I am not 'loving the Lord my God with all my heart and with all my soul and with all my strength and with all my mind—and my neighbor as myself' (Luke 10:27)." In a recent article in the *Trumpet* titled "The Sin of Idleness," you can read the biblical quote: "Behold, this was the iniquity [or sin] of thy sister Sodom, pride, fullness of bread, and *abundance of idleness* was in her and in her daughters, neither did she strengthen the hand of the poor and needy" (Ezekiel 16:49). There are hundreds of websites that describe wasting time as a sin. Could it be that somewhere in our cultural psyche we feel guilty and even immoral for simply taking time off from work, simply letting our minds lie fallow, simply wasting time?

The biblical notion of idleness has been defined in terms of what it is *not*. Idleness is not work. And work, according to the Bible, is the bidding of God: "Christ biddeth us pray 'the Lord of the harvest to send forth labourers into his harvest.' " The Bible celebrates work, so that not working (i.e., idleness) is considered a sin. Similarly, the ancient Roman idea of *otium* was defined, first and foremost, as what it was not. It was time spent away from work. I suggest that we should think of the time spent in creative thought, in quiet reflection and contemplation, in mental replenishment, in consolidation of our identity and values in *positive* terms—not as what it is not, but what it is. It is time to restore our psychological well-being. It is time to promote growth as human beings. It is time to unleash our imaginations. It is time to protect our sanity. It is time to understand who we are and who we are becoming. "Wasting time" engaged in the activities I've described is far from immoral uselessness. It may be the most important occupation of our minds.

8 Half Mind

In 2016, the Harvard biologist emeritus and naturalist E. O. Wilson published *Half-Earth: Our Planet's Fight for Life*, in which he proposes that half the earth's surface be designated and protected as conservation land. The human destruction of our environment and the natural world is a fairly recent phenomenon in the history of human civilization. In the sixteenth century, Spanish invaders began spouting large amounts of lead dust into the air after they seized the mines of the Incas and instituted new means of extracting silver. Further pollution, deforestation, and the elimination of species through human exploitation began with the Industrial Revolution and the increasing demand for energy and other resources. That demand has only accelerated. Climate scientists have concluded that the main driver of global warming since 1950 has been the dramatic increase in carbon dioxide from the burning of fossil fuels. Starting in the late 1960s, Brazil began cutting down and burning trees in the Amazon rain forest at an increasing rate. By 2013, the country had cleared eighteen percent of the forest. According to the World Wide Fund for Nature, human beings have destroyed more than thirty percent of forests and the marine ecosystem just since 1970.

It is probably true that no single individual or society has intentionally set out to decimate the natural world. The destruction has been an unintended consequence of population growth, the desire for increased material wealth and comfort, and the associated need for more energy. The destruction has also been driven by the inexorable imperative of capitalism and the powerful desire of certain individuals to increase their personal wealth. Wilson's proposal might be difficult to achieve, but it represents a recognition of the importance of our natural environment and the forces that threaten it.

The destruction of our inner selves via the wired world is an even more recent phenomenon, and one more subtle than the destruction of the natural world. The loss of slowness, of time for reflection and contemplation, of privacy and solitude, of silence, of the ability to sit quietly in a chair for fifteen minutes without external stimulation—all have happened quickly and almost invisibly. A hundred and fifty years ago, the telephone didn't exist. Fifty years ago, the Internet didn't exist. Twenty-five years ago, Google didn't exist. As I mentioned earlier, just since 1985 the speed of information transfer has increased from about a thousand bits per second to about one billion bits per second today. The walking speed of pedestrians in Singapore has increased by a whopping thirty percent since the mid-1990s.

Some of the forces that have driven these changes are the same as those that have led to the destruction of our environment: the desire to improve material wealth and comfort, and economic ambition. In addition, there is the glittering lure of technology as an end in itself, without consideration of the true quality of life. As with the destruction of the environment, no one intended to rob us of our interior lives. Each of us once swallowed that first bite of the wired world, then the second. Then we were addicted. Soon, we couldn't remember what we had lost. Our children, of course, were born into the wired world, never knowing any other way of life. All this in the name of "progress."

The situation is dire. Just as with global warming, we may already be near the point of no return. Invisibly, almost without notice, we are losing ourselves. We are losing our ability to know who we are and what is important to us. We are creating a global machine in which each of us is a mindless and reflexive cog, relentlessly driven by the speed, noise, and artificial urgency of the wired world.

What can we do? Somehow, we need to create a new "habit of mind," as individuals and as a society. We need a mental attitude that values and protects stillness, privacy, solitude, slowness, personal reflection; that honors the inner self; that allows each of us to wander about without schedule within our own minds.

Wilson's proposal is bold. I would like to make a similarly bold proposal: that half our waking minds be designated and saved for quiet reflection. Otherwise, we are destroying our inner selves and our creative capacities. Of course, our minds are not geographical territory like the surface of the earth, but different moments throughout the day can be devoted to contemplation and stillness, free from the external world. Isn't our creativity, our inner equilibrium, our ability to know ourselves and where we are going worth at least half of our minds? Half Mind, we might call the idea.

How do we develop a contemplative habit of mind? It is not easy, especially when the outside world is screaming otherwise. Twenty years ago, a friend of mine who taught high school in Arlington, Massachusetts, started something new with her students. At the beginning of each class, she rang a bell and asked the students to remain silent for four minutes. As she wrote later, "I explained [to my students] that I felt our school days were too fast-paced and filled with noise, that silence could help us leave behind the previous class, and prepare to be present for this one. That it was a time to clear our heads. I said we were aiming for internal and external stillness." The results were miraculous, she told me. Both she and the students were calmer and more centered. In subsequent years, her students did not want her to give up the bell and the minutes of silence.

In recent years, numerous organizations, such as Mindful Schools and the Mindful Education Institute, have been created to introduce periods of quiet and meditation into primary and secondary schools. As one particular example, in 2015 Stacy Sims, a mind-body educator, started a program called Mindful Music Moments, part of City Silence, in which students listen to four minutes of classical music during the morning announcement period—similar to the idea of my friend in Massachusetts. Mindful Music Moments now operates in sixty-five K-12 schools, camps, and social service organizations, most of them in Cincinnati.

To develop new habits of mind, different groups must use different methods. I have some recommendations, which should be viewed as starting points rather than comprehensive solutions to the problem:

- For K-12 students, a ten-minute period of silence sometime during the school day. Such a period could occur while students are in homeroom. Students could quietly write down thoughts in a notebook during this time. Different schools have different cultures, and each school will know how best to institute this period of silence.

- For college students, "introspective intensive" courses created by each academic department. Each student would be required to take at least one such course each semester. Introspective courses, while based in the particular subject matter of the department—for example, history or chemistry, would have a reduced load of reading and assignments and encourage students to use the free time to reflect on what they are learning and relate it to their lives and life goals. Such reflections might be expressed in essays or other creative activities.

- In the workplace, a "quiet room" or similar space where employees are permitted and encouraged to spend a half hour each day meditating, reflecting, or simply being silent. Smartphones and computers would not be allowed in the quiet room. This period of quiet would not be part of the regular lunch break. A number of companies have already instituted meditation as part of the workday.

- For families, an "unplugged" hour during the evening, perhaps during dinner, in which all phones, smart-phones, computers, and other devices are turned off. Dinner should not be gulped down but should be a time for quiet conversation.

- Individuals should think about how they spend their time each day and try to build in a half hour away from the wired world, such as taking a walk while unplugged, reading, or simply sitting quietly.

- For society as a whole, mandated "screen-free zones" in public spaces, where digital devices are forbidden, and labor laws in which workers are guaranteed a half hour each day of quiet time at the workplace.

These measures might seem trivial or ineffectual, but I believe they would be part of an effort to increase awareness of the importance of our contemplative selves and to develop new habits of mind. New habits of mind take time. Cigarettes were once positively embedded in American culture. They were promoted as a pleasure, a sign of sophistication and coolness, even a symbol of masculinity. Advertisements showed business tycoons, movie stars, and even athletes smoking cigarettes. Then, beginning in the 1950s, there was a slow but growing recognition of the health hazards of cigarettes. Since the mid-1960s, the percentage of cigarette smokers has dropped by more than half. We have developed a new habit of mind toward smoking. I believe that we can develop a new habit of mind toward the wired world, but it will take time. First, we will need to recognize the danger.

I continue to be haunted by the picture of the despondent teenager on the cover of *Time*. Certainly, she and her generation should take some of the responsibility for their addiction to the wired world at the expense of their inner selves. But shouldn't we who created that world take more responsibility? Of course, we are victims ourselves, but we are also the perpetrators. We are both prisoners and jailors. Don't we owe that young woman, and all of our children, a world in which their contemplative lives are valued and supported? Don't we owe it to ourselves?

Although changing habits of mind is difficult, it can be done. It is within the power of each of us as individuals and as families and as workers to make changes in our way of living to restore our inner lives. All we need is recognition of the problem, and a personal commitment. With a little determination, each of us can find a half hour a day to waste time. When we do so, we give ourselves a gift. It is a gift to our spirit. It is an honoring of that quiet, whispering voice. It is a liberation from the cage of the wired world. It is freedom. Decades ago, when I was that boy walking home from school through the woods, following turtles as they slowly lumbered down a dirt path, wasting hours as I watched tadpoles in the shallows or the sway of water grasses in the wind, I was free. We cannot return to that world, nor would we necessarily want to, but we can create some of that space within our world today. We can create a preserve within our own minds.

ACKNOWLEDGMENTS

For their helpful comments and/or inspirations, I am happy to thank Nancy Andreasen, Tejinder Billing, Lucile Burt, Ross Peterson, Paul Schechter, Sherry Turkle, and Mark Wolf.

I also thank Michelle Quint at TED Books for her superb editing of this book.

NOTES

A VILLAGE IN CAMBODIA

8   *Gustav Mahler routinely took*: Alma Mahler, *Gustav Mahler: Memories and Letters*, ed. Donald Mitchell, trans. Basil Creighton (New York: Viking Press, 1969).

8   *Carl Jung did his most creative thinking*: Carl Jung, *Memories, Dreams, Reflections*, ed. Aniela Jaffé, trans. Richard and Clara Winston (New York: Vintage Books, 1989).

8   *Gertrude Stein wandered about the countryside*: See the chapter "The Free-Grazing Mind" and the second note to that chapter below.

8   *"For me it is unquestionable that our thinking goes on"*: Albert Einstein, *Albert Einstein: Philosopher-Scientist*, ed. Paul Arthur Schilpp (La Salle, Illinois: Open Court, 1949), 7–9.

9   *"When a monk has gone into an empty place"*: The Dhammapada, in *Buddhist Meditation: An Anthology of Texts from the Pāli Canon*, trans. Sarah Shaw (London: Routledge, 2006), 24.

THE GRID

10   *from 2010 to 2015 the fraction of adolescents*: "Teen Depression and Anxiety: Why the Kids Are Not Alright," *Time*, November 7, 2016, 50. See also "Major Depression Among Adolescents," National Institute of Mental Health: https://www.nimh.nih.gov/health/statistics/prevalence/major-depression-among-adolescents.shtml.

11   *"in a cauldron of stimulus"*: Janis Whitlock quoted in "Teen Depression and Anxiety: Why the Kids Are Not Alright," *Time*, 47.

11   *According to a recent Pew survey*: Pew Research Center's Internet & American Life Project, April 26–May 22, 2011, Spring Tracking Survey.

11   *"there is no firm line between their real and online worlds"*: "Teen Depression and Anxiety: Why the Kids Are Not Alright," *Time*, 47. See also Marion K. Underwood and Robert Faris, "#Being Thirteen: Social Media and the Hidden World of Young Adolescents' Peer Culture," 2015: https://assets.documentcloud.org/documents/2448422/being-13-report.pdf.

11   *"terror of aloneness"*: interview with Ross Peterson by Alan Lightman, March 19, 2017.

12   *In her new book* iGen: Jean Twenge, *iGen: Why Today's Super-Connected Kids Are Growing Up Less Rebellious, More Tolerant, Less Happy—and Completely Unprepared for Adulthood—and What That Means for the Rest of Us* (New York: Simon and Schuster, 2017). See also Jean Twenge, "Have Smartphones Destroyed a Generation?" *The Atlantic*, September 2017.

12   *survey by investment firm Piper Jaffray*: Piper Jaffray surveyed 5,500 American teenagers. See http://www.piperjaffray.com/3col.aspx?id=4359.

12-13 *"I know I shouldn't, but I just can't help it"*: "Have Smartphones Destroyed a Generation?"

13   *"Technology proposes itself as the architect"*: Sherry Turkle, *Alone Together: Why We Expect More from Technology and Less from Each Other* (New York: Basic Books, 2011), 1.

13   *Surveys show that since the advent*: "Have Smartphones Destroyed a Generation?"

16   *psychologists at the University of Virginia and Harvard*: Timothy D. Wilson, David A. Reinhard, Erin C. Westgate et al., "Just think: The challenges of the disengaged mind," *Science* 345, no. 6192 (2014): 75-77.

17   *In her book* Distracted: Maggie Jackson, *Distracted: The Erosion of Attention and the Coming Dark Age* (New York: Prometheus Books, 2008).

17   *In an article titled*: Gloria Mark, Victor M. Gonzalez, and Justin Harris, "No Task Left Behind? Examining the Nature of Fragmented Work," *Proceedings of the SIGCHI Conference on Human Factors in Computer Systems* (2005), 321-30.

THE RUSH AND THE HEAVE

21   *study by the University of Hertfordshire*: Fiona MacRae, "Pace of Life Speeds Up as Study Reveals We're Walking Faster Than Ever," *Daily Mail*, May 2, 2007, http://www.dailymail.co.uk/sciencetech/article-452046/Pace-life-speeds -study-reveals-walking-faster-ever.html. See also the British Council press release "International Experiment Proves Pace of Life Is Speeding Up by 10%," March 25, 2007, http://www.richardwiseman.com/resources/Pace%20of%20 LifePR.pdf, and Kate Kelland, "World's Cities Step Up Pace of Life in the Fast Lane," Reuters, May 2, 2007.

21   *in a book titled*: George Beard, *American Nervousness: Its Causes and Consequences* (New York: Putnam, 1881).

22   *Fifty years ago*: Gary S. Becker, "A Theory of the Allocation of Time," *The Economic Journal* 75, no. 299 (September 1965): 493–517.

23   *According to the Bureau of Labor Statistics, productivity has*: Shawn Sprague, "What can labor productivity tell us about the U.S. economy?" *Beyond the Numbers* 3, no. 12 (May 2014), https://www.bls.gov/opub/btn/volume-3/what -can-labor-productivity-tell-us-about-the-us-economy.htm.

23   *"creates an urgency to make every moment count"*: Harry Triandis quoted in "Why is everyone so busy?" *The Economist*, December 20, 2014, http://www .economist.com/news/christmas-specials/21636612-time-poverty-problem -partly-perception-and-partly-distribution-why.

23   *A recent survey of 483 professionals*: Jennifer J. Deal, "Welcome to the 72-Hour Work Week," *Harvard Business Review*, September 12, 2013, https://hbr.org/2013/09 /welcome-to-the-72-hour-work-we.

23   *A study by legal scholar*: M. Cathleen Kaveny, "Billable Hours in Ordinary Time: A Theological Critique of the Instrumentalization of Time in Professional Life," *Loyola University Chicago Law Journal* 33, no. 1 (Summer 2002): 173–220.

24   *In a fascinating experiment*: Sanford E. DeVoe and Julian House, "Time, money, and happiness: How does putting a price on time affect our ability to smell the roses?" *Journal of Experimental Social Psychology* 48, no. 2 (March 2012): 466–74.

26   *According to a survey by the Associated Press*: http://cdn.halfofus.com /wp-content/uploads/2013/10/mtvU-AP-College-Stress-and-Mental-Health -Poll-Executive-Summary.pdf.

26   *A survey of over 350,000 students*: Kay Cooperman, "Record Numbers of the Nation's Freshmen Feel High Degree of Stress, UCLA Study Finds," *UCLA Newsroom*, January 24, 2000, http://newsroom.ucla.edu/releases /Record-Numbers-of-the-Nation-s-355.

26   *"This [trend] is a reflection of"*: Cooperman, "Record Numbers of the Nation's Freshmen Feel High Degree of Stress, UCLA Study Finds."

27   *"Here's a quick look into a normal day for me"*: McKenna Bulkley, "Of Course I'm Stressed, I'm in College," *Huffington Post*, April 21, 2015.

27-8   *"despite the tremendous educational potential of the information age"*: Adam Peck, "Overloaded with information, students need critical thinking skills," *University World News*, February 26, 2012.

28   *"Like many parents, I feel an immense amount"*: Rachel Garlinghouse, "The Best Gifts I Can Give My Children to Ensure Their Success," *Huffington Post*, May 4, 2015.

29   *"Our life is frittered away by detail"*: Henry David Thoreau, *Walden* (New York: Norton, 1951), 106.

30   *"We do not ride on the railroad"*: Thoreau, *Walden*, 108.

PLAY

34   *"the benefit play accords each child"*: Brian Sutton-Smith, "Play Theory: A Personal Journey and New Thoughts," *American Journal of Play* 1, no. 1 (Summer 2008): 118–19.

34   *"These perceptions and uses may violate"*: Signe Juhl Møller, "Imagination, Playfulness, and Creativity in Children's Play with Different Toys," *American Journal of Play* 7, no. 3 (Spring 2015): 324.

35   *"Play is the total of all the spontaneous"*: Valerie Van Cauwenberghe quoted in "Defining Play," by Stephen Hurley, EdCan Network, Canadian Educational Association (CEA), January 22, 2015, https://www.edcan.ca/articles /defining-play/.

35   *"Play allows children to use their creativity"*: Kenneth R. Ginsburg, "The Importance of Play in Promoting Healthy Child Development and Maintaining Strong Parent-Child Bonds," *Pediatrics* 119, no. 1 (January 2007).

35   *A similar conclusion has been reached*: Kathy Hirsh-Pasek, Roberta Michnick Golinkoff et al., *A Mandate for Playful Learning in Preschool* (New York: Oxford University Press, 2009).

35   *Jihae Shin, an assistant professor*: Shin's experiment is described in "Why I Taught Myself to Procrastinate," by Adam Grant, *New York Times Sunday Review*, January 16, 2016.

37   *a few minutes in the lives of some young crows*: "Crows Playing Swinging from a Branch," uploaded August 20, 2011, https://www.youtube.com/ watch?v=YbdNtC4V3IM.

37   *Psychologist Anthony Pellegrini*: For more on the work of Pellegrini, see his *The Role of Play in Human Development* (New York: Oxford University Press, 2009), and "The Role of Recess in Children's Cognitive Performance and School Adjustment" by Anthony D. Pellegrini and Catherine M. Bohn, *Educational Researcher* 34, no. 1 (January 2005): 13–19.

39 *"Let the best robot win"*: See Flowers in action at https://www.youtube.com
    /watch?v=9BFDotuTSB8.

39 *"We worked hard, toiling late into the night, hunched over our benches"*: 2.70
    Introduction to Design, Contest 1995 (Pebble Beach): http://web.mit.edu/2.70
    /www_OLD/contest/results.html.

THE FREE-GRAZING MIND

41 *"At Caltech, every time one of the professors walked by"*: Paul Schechter, interview
    with Alan Lightman, November 11, 2016.

42 *"Miss Stein gets up every morning"*: Janet Flanner, James Thurber, and Harold
    Ross, "Tender Buttons," *The New Yorker*, October 13, 1934.

43 *"The night before Easter Sunday"*: Otto Loewi, "An Autobiographical Sketch,"
    Perspectives in Biology and Medicine 4 (1960): 3–25. The quote can be found on 17–18.

43 *"I'm up at six in the morning"*: Hollis Alpert, *Fellini: A Life* (New York: Paragon
    House, 1988), 264.

43 *"For fifteen days, I strove to prove"*: Henri Poincaré, *The Foundations of Science*,
    trans. George Bruce Halsted (New York: The Science Press, 1913), 387.

44 *German psychiatrist and physicist named*: For a good biography of Berger and
    his work see David Millett, "Hans Berger: From Psychic Energy to the EEG,"
    Perspectives in Biology and Medicine 44, no. 4 (Autumn 2001): 522–42.

46 *coined the term "defult mode"*: For Marcus Raichle's discussion of the default
    mode, see Marcus E. Raichle, Ann Mary MacLeod, Abraham Z. Snyder et al., "A
    default mode of brain function," *Proceedings of the National Academy of Sciences*
    98, no. 2 (January 2001): 676–82.

46 *commonly called free association*: For more on Nancy Andreasen's work: See
    N. C. Andreasen, D. S. O'Leary, T. Cizadlo et al., "Remembering the past:
    Two facets of episodic memory explored with positron emission tomography,"
    American Journal of Psychiatry 152, no. 11 (1995): 1576–85, and Nancy C.
    Andreasen, "A Journey into chaos: Creativity and the unconscious," *Mens Sana
    Monographs* 9, no. 1 (2011): 42–53.

47 *"[T]he truth is I write by ear"*: E. B. White, "Author's Note" in *Essays of E. B.
    White* (New York: Harper, 1977), 319.

47   *"Unsatisfied wishes are the driving power behind fantasies"*: Sigmund Freud, "The Relation of the Poet to Daydreaming" (1908), in *The Standard Edition of the Complete Psychological Works of Sigmund Freud*, trans. and ed. James Strachey, vol. 9 (London: Hogarth Press, 1956-1974); reprinted in *Twentieth-Century Theories of Art*, ed. James M. Thompson (Ottawa: Carleton University Press, 1990), 126.

49   *The psychologist J. Nina Lieberman*: J. Nina Lieberman, "Playfulness and divergent thinking: An investigation of their relationship at the kindergarten level," *The Journal of Genetic Psychology* 107, no. 2 (1965): 219-24.

53   *creative thinking follows a series of stages*: Graham Wallas, *The Art of Thought* (Kent, England: Solis Press, 2014; originally published in 1926).

53   *"[T]he material has obviously been incubating"*: T. S. Eliot, *The Use of Poetry and the Use of Criticism* (Faber and Faber, 1933), 144.

54   *"I am a believer in unconscious cerebration"*: Alexander Graham Bell, interviewed by Orison Swett Marden, in Marden, *How They Succeeded: Life Stories of Successful Men Told by Themselves* (Boston: Lothrop, Lee & Shepard, 1901), 33.

54   *Some years ago, I did a study*: Alan Lightman, *The Discoveries: Great Breakthroughs in 20th-Century Science* (New York: Pantheon Books, 2005), and Lightman, "Moments of Truth," *New Scientist*, November 19, 2005, 36.

57   *Researcher Kyung Hee Kim*: Kyung Hee Kim, "The Creativity Crisis: The Decrease in Creative Thinking Scores on the Torrance Tests of Creative Thinking," *Creativity Research Journal* 23, no. 4 (November 2011): 285-95.

58   *"[C]hildren have become less emotionally expressive"*: Kyung Hee Kim, "The Creativity Crisis," 292.

DOWNTIME AND REPLENISHMENT

61   *numerous studies have suggested:* Scientific studies on the benefits of meditation and mindfulness are often associated with the name Jon Kabat-Zinn. Kabat-Zinn is the author of many popular books on the subject, has conducted research himself, and founded the Stress Reduction Clinic and the Center for Mindfulness in Medicine, Health Care, and Society at the University of Massachusetts Medical School. One of his best-known books on the subject is *Full Catastrophe Living* (Delacorte Press, 1990).

61   *to mention only one:* Ruth Baer, Emily Lykins, and Jessica Peters, "Mindfulness and self-compassion as predictors of psychological wellbeing in long-term meditators and matched nonmeditators," *The Journal of Positive Psychology* 7, no. 3 (April 2012): 230-38.

61   *alterations in brain and immune function produced by mindfulness meditation*:
R. J. Davidson, J. Kabat-Zinn, J. Schumacher et al., *Psychosomatic Medicine* 65,
no. 4 (July/August 2003): 564–70.

65   *Emily Dickinson compared stillness*: See "The Difference Between Despair,"
Poem 305.

In my recent book *Searching for Stars on an Island in Maine*, I have argued that
the Self is largely an illusion. What I mean by this is that the strong feeling that
the Self—our "I"-ness—is endowed with some supernatural and mystical quality,
some magnificent nonmaterial essence, is an illusion. I believe that the brain,
and all the thoughts and feelings that arise from it, is purely material. What
we label as our Self, our awareness and consciousness, is a name we give to the
particular sensations produced by the electrical and chemical activity of our
hundred billion neurons. That being said, the sensations are nonetheless real.
Our thoughts are real. Our existence as a living organism is real. And therefore
we still must organize our thoughts and actions so as to nurture and protect
ourselves and our sense of who we are. Thus the material basis of the Self, in the
brain, in no way contradicts the discussion in this chapter.

68   *One of the first experimental studies*: Research on sleep by Maria Mikhailovna
Manaseina, and by Lamberto Daddi and Giulio Tarozzi. See M. Bentivoglio and
G. Grassi-Zucconi, "The pioneering experimental studies on sleep deprivation,"
Sleep 20, no. 7 (July 1997): 570–76.

CHRONOS AND KAIROS

74   *"I realized people [in the United States]"*: interview with Tejinder Billing by Alan
Lightman, October 21, 2016, and also in "Time—or Lack Thereof—Impacts
Stress Levels," *Rowan Today*, October 21, 2010.

74   *In research on time use*: T. K. Billing, R. S. Bhagat, A. Lammel, and K. Leonard,
"Temporal Orientation and Its Relationships with Organizationally
Valued Outcomes: Results from a 14-Country Investigation," in *Quod Erat
Demonstrandum: From Herodotus' Ethnographic Journeys to Cross-Cultural
Research*, eds. A. Gari & K. Mylanos (Athens: Atrapos Editions, 2009): 211–31.

74   *"it is common to accept with indifference"*: Ibid, 213.

75   *a fascinating book*: George Levine, *A Geography of Time: The Temporal
Misadventures of a Social Psychologist* (New York: Basic Books, 1997).

76   *the sociologist Juliet Schor*: Juliet Schor, *The Overworked American: The
Unexpected Decline of Leisure* (New York: Basic Books, 1992).

79 *a short novel about time*: Alan Lightman, *Einstein's Dreams* (New York: Pantheon Books, 1993).

80 Westminster Shorter Catechism: See, for example, http://www.epc.org /file/mainmenu/beliefs/catechisms/short/0e417539_westminster-shorter -catechism.pdf.

81 *"The greater and more excellent any man's work"*: *The Practical Works of the Rev. Richard Baxter*, vol. 12 (London: James Duncan, 1830), Chapter XVII, 463. See https://ia600300.us.archive.org/32/items/practicalworksr02baxtgoog /practicalworksr02baxtgoog.pdf.

81 *"Wasting time is a sin"*: See "Is Wasting Time a Sin?" *Life of a Steward*, http://www.lifeofasteward.com/is-wasting-time-a-sin/.

81 *"Behold, this was the iniquity"*: "The Sin of Idleness," *The Trumpet*, the Philadelphia Church of God, https://www.thetrumpet.com/1119-the-sin-of-idleness.

HALF MIND

83 *E. O. Wilson published*: E. O. Wilson, *Half-Earth: Our Planet's Fight for Life* (New York: Liveright, 2016).

83 *Climate scientists have concluded*: See "When Did Anthropogenic Global Warming Begin?" *Watts Up with That?* March 29, 2014, https://wattsupwiththat. com/2014/03/29/when-did-anthropogenic-global-warming-begin/.

83 *By 2013, the country had cleared*: See "Tragedy and Transformation: Deforestation in the Amazon," *EDF Voices: People on the Planet*, Environmental Defense Fund, March 20, 2013, https://www.edf.org/blog/2013/11/14 /tragedy-and-transformation-deforestation-amazon.

83 *According to the World Wide Fund*: See the "Living Planet Report 2016," http://wwf.panda.org/about_our_earth/all_publications/lpr_2016/.

86 *remain silent for four minutes*: The high school teacher is Lucile Burt, who taught at Arlington High School in Massachusetts. The quotes come from an unpublished essay. My interview with her took place on June 16, 2017.

ABOUT THE AUTHOR

Alan Lightman is a physicist, novelist, and essayist. He was educated at Princeton University and at the California Institute of Technology, where he received a Ph.D. in theoretical physics. Before coming to MIT, he was on the faculty of Harvard University. At MIT, Lightman was one of the first people to receive dual faculty appointments in science and in the humanities and was John Burchard Professor of Humanities before becoming Professor of the Practice of the Humanities.

Lightman is the author of five novels, several collections of essays, a book-length narrative poem, a memoir, and several books on science. His writing has appeared in *The Atlantic*, *Granta*, *Harper's*, *The New Yorker*, *The New York Review of Books*, *Nautilus*, and *Salon*, among other publications. His novel *Einstein's Dreams* was an international best seller and has been translated into thirty languages. His novel *The Diagnosis* was a finalist for the 2000 National Book Award in fiction. He is an elected member of the American Academy of Arts and Sciences and has won numerous other awards, including five honorary doctoral degrees. Lightman is also the founder of the Harpswell Foundation, which works to advance a new generation of women leaders in Southeast Asia.

WATCH ALAN LIGHTMAN'S TED TALK

Alan Lightman's TED Talk, available for free at TED.com, is the companion to *In Praise of Wasting Time*.

RELATED TALKS

Pico Iyer
The Art of Stillness
The place that travel writer Pico Iyer would most like to go? Nowhere. In a counterintuitive and lyrical meditation, Iyer takes a look at the incredible insight that comes with taking time for stillness. In our world of constant movement and distraction, he teases out strategies we all can use to take back a few minutes out of every day, or a few days out of every season. It's the talk for anyone who feels overwhelmed by the demands of our world.

Matthieu Ricard
The Habit of Happiness
What is happiness, and how can we all get some? Biochemist-turned–Buddhist monk Matthieu Ricard says we can train our minds in habits of well-being, to generate a true sense of serenity and fulfillment.

Stefan Sagmeister
The Power of Time Off
Every seven years, designer Stefan Sagmeister closes his New York studio for a yearlong sabbatical to rejuvenate and refresh his creative outlook. He explains the often overlooked value of time off and shows the innovative projects inspired by his time in Bali.

Elizabeth Gilbert
Your Elusive Creative Genius
Elizabeth Gilbert muses on the impossible things we expect from artists and geniuses—and shares the radical idea that, instead of the rare person "being" a genius, all of us "have" a genius. It's a funny, personal, and surprisingly moving talk.

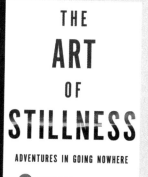

How to Fix a Broken Heart
by Guy Winch

A broken heart is unmistakable. We think of nothing else. We feel nothing else. We care about nothing else. Yet we know so little about how to deal with it. With great wisdom and empathy, psychologist Guy Winch explores how different our lives and our society would be if we better understood this unique emotional pain.

The Art of Stillness
by Pico Iyer

An unexpected truth from a celebrated travel writer: Stillness just might be the ultimate adventure. Pico Iyer reveals how stillness can act as a creative catalyst, and advocates for a way of living that counters the frenetic design of our modern lives.

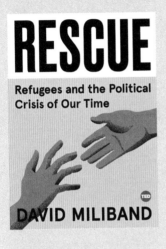

Rescue
by David Miliband

We are in the midst of a global refugee crisis. Sixty-five million people are fleeing for their lives. The choices are urgent, not just for them but for all of us. What can we possibly do to help?

The Misfit's Manifesto
by Lidia Yuknavitch

By reclaiming and celebrating the word *misfit*, this manifesto makes a powerful case for not fitting in—for recognizing the beauty, and difficulty, in forging an original path.

ABOUT TED BOOKS

TED Books are small books about big ideas. They're short enough to read in a single sitting, but long enough to delve deep into a topic. The wide-ranging series covers everything from architecture to business, space travel to love, and is perfect for anyone with a curious mind and an expansive love of learning.

Each TED Book is paired with a related TED Talk, available online at TED.com. The books pick up where the talks leave off. An eighteen-minute speech can plant a seed or spark the imagination, but many talks create a need to go deeper, to learn more, to tell a longer story. TED Books fill this need.